First Name
Variants

THIRD EDITION

Alan Bardsley

Published by
The Federation of Family History Societies (Publications) Ltd.,
Units 15-16, Chesham Industrial Centre, Oram Street,
Bury, Lancashire BL9 6EN

First published (privately) 1992
Second edition 1996
Third edition 2003

ISBN 1-86006-177-X

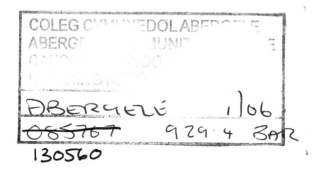
Printed by and bound by the Alden Group, Oxford OX2 0EF

Contents

Introduction   4

Sources   4

Sorting methods   4

Development and history of variants   6

How to use this book   8

Acknowledgements   9

Bibliography   10

Addresses   11

Index: First Names with codes   13

Index: Codes giving variants   55

Introduction

When searching for records of particular individuals in original documents or indexes most researchers would be familiar with an Elizabeth appearing as a Betty or Bessy. They may be less familiar with it appearing as Tissy or Veta and there are at least 230 other ways that Elizabeth has been recorded. Over time first names have suffered from many variations both accidentally and deliberately introduced, sometimes making it difficult to track a particular person. This book is a compilation of first name diminutives and variants and links together all those that have a relationship.

The primary aim has been to cover the 17th to 19th century usage when, due to the limited literacy, the written name adopted many forms. The coverage is for the English speaking world of that period together with the commoner Welsh, Irish and Scottish links.

Sources
The usage of names in this compilation has been derived from two main sources. First the 2% sample of the 1851 United Kingdom census and secondly the, mainly unpublished, records of myself and individual researchers noted in the acknowledgements. These records comprise some 700,000 usages. The analysis and linking has been done using the above records and, mainly from an etymological viewpoint, the publications noted in the bibliography.

The final compilation consists of some 8000 variants linked to 1300 standard names.

Sorting Methods
In order to link one name to another some method of sorting and coding has to be adopted. A well known method used to identify surname variants is the Soundex system which codes the

consonants at the beginning of a name. This fails with first names because, as will be seen later, syncope, rhyming and letter changing diminutives significantly alter the consonant structure. When the miss-hearings, spelling mistakes and common transcription errors are added to the logically derived diminutives it is hard to arrive at an automatic sorting system which works. I have adopted a purely manual system and studied each entry individually to establish its links. Later workers may be able to take this further and develop, particularly for computer searching, automatic methods.

The primary aim is to help to identify individuals where there is a possibility that their name may have been modified. This purpose has overridden any etymological rules. Therefore some names will be linked that do not have the same roots but only became related because of, say, a common phonetic transcription. Whilst the majority of links do have an etymological provenance the reader should beware that some may not and reference should be made to the literature in the bibliography for a study of this aspect.

For convenience in discussion each of the linked groups has been allocated a standard name. For example Elizabeth is used as a standard name for all its variants. The temptation to say that this is then the "correct" name for any individual should be avoided. Many a person has been baptised Betty, and surely that was what was intended, not Elizabeth. We are concerned with whether they may have subsequently become known as Tissy or Lizzy or even erroneously back transcribed as Elizabeth by some previous worker. Each individual bears whatever name they do from their history, we cannot gainsay that today.

Many first names for males and females have common roots and over time, either by miss-spelling or by deliberate usage, have been used indiscriminately for either. Today one perhaps might think one knows the gender of a Francis and a Frances, the subtlety of the difference was certainly not apparent in less literate days. Hence no distinction is made between possible male and female usage and other evidence should always be considered before drawing any gender conclusions.

Certain diminutives may be used for more than one standard name. For example Tina for Christina, Clementina, Valentina etc. In these cases the diminutive has been allocated to the standard with the most common usage and a cross reference given to the others.

Development and History of Variants

Names have been attached to individuals from the beginning of recorded time. The Romans developed a multiple name system using family group or branch names with the addition of a praenomen for males from a limited list of about 36 names. England in the main found it sufficient to use only one name until around the 13th century. At this stage the population outgrew the available number of single names and the combination of a first name and surname rapidly developed. The surname being accepted as the family group part of the name to be passed on by the male line.

The rich sources of English as a language have all contributed words to use as names. The early tradition of naming was to use words of good augury and strength. For example:-

Edwin	Old English	happy (rich) & friend
Margaret	Greek	pearl
Gerard	Old German	spear & hard

It should not be forgotten that in the beginning names were words in every day use, not, as they are now considered, special name words. A similar, perhaps more recently familiar, situation arose with the development of surnames whose origins are rapidly being forgotten in every day use. We all still know where Smith came from but Fletcher, the arrow supplier, is becoming less understood.

The practice of usage of good words was taken up again later by the Puritans in the 16-17th centuries and the use of such as Patience and Faith has a strange feel to it today precisely because these are normal words still in common use.

In the dark ages England struggled along with its Nordic, Gaelic and Latin legacies. With the arrival of the Normans all was swept aside and either because it was fashionable or prudent the conquerors names instantly became the most popular. William, Richard and Ralph were the most favoured but in reality most of the Norman names were only French variants of the polyglot names that England had absorbed from centuries before.

As the Church came to dominate peoples lives in the 13th century scriptural names came into prominence. For the next 500 years William, John, and Thomas and Elizabeth, Mary and Anne were used by 50% of the population. Less significant introductions were during the Reformation in the 16th century causing a revival of Old Testament names aided by the Puritan developments noted before. Finally, as surnames were introduced they also began to be used as first names. This was particularly so in the 19th century where aristocratic surnames such as Percy, Sydney and Neville were popular.

The introduction of first names from entirely new roots is extremely rare after the 17th century. In current times there is an even greater variants explosion as people exploit their educated ingenuity on our store of name words.

These were the basic sources of what was now a rich panoply of name words. It still remained for scribes and the populace to make what they would of them.

In early times the degree of literacy dictated the development of mainly phonetic variants.

> Esther, Ester, Hester
> Henry, Henrie, Henery
> Lewis, Lewys, Louis
> Ralph, Rauf, Ralf, Rolf

Scribes also adopted common abbreviations such as Ricd (Richard) and Wm (William). As the population grew, and perhaps due to further pressure to identify one Elizabeth or William from the many that there were, the full development modes of language started to be applied.

Apocope or syncope, where parts of a word are dropped,
William, Eliza**beth**, **Eliza**beth, Frederick

Rhyming and letter changing,

> **Ric**hard, Ric, Dick, Hick
> **Ric**hard, Rich, Hitch
> **Rob**ert, Rob, Bob, Dob, Hob, Nob

Endings,

> Mary, Marion, Mariot, Marriete
> Margaret, Meg, Meggie, Meggy, Peggy
> Janet, Janot, Janett, Janeta, Janis

The largest growth in variants occurred in the 19th century as the population soared and literacy was still limited. The use of variants shows interesting patterns. Up to the end of the 19th century it would be quite common for variants to be used in registers, wills, court records, censuses and other contemporary reports. Latterly the original birth registration name tends to be used in formal records but there is still common use of variants in casual records such as newspapers. These are however from a very limited range of a few well known examples such as, Betty, Bill, Jack, Bert. Many variants have now come to be established as names in their own right. The Lisa and Isabel variants of Elizabeth for example would not now be considered as linked. Betty however, whilst used as a baptism name in the 19th century would now only be seen as a diminutive.

How to use this book

To find the group or standard name for a variant first look up the variant in the index "First Names with Codes". This gives a three letter code for the variant, e.g. **Oliva** gives **oli**. Then look up **oli** in the index "Codes giving Variants". This gives, amongst others:-

oli	Livie	hel
	Nola	ola
	Noll	
	Nollie	
	Oliff	
	Oliva	
	Oliver	

The second column shows the variants that may have been adopted for Oliva and, in bold, shows the suggested standard name. As was noted before some variants have been used for more than one standard name. The third column gives the codes for these possible links. In this example with hel (Helen) which has Nell, Nellie amongst its variants and with ola (Olave) for Olaf. These links can get extremely complicated and, if a simple review does not help, the reader is advised to study the bibliography for the full etymology.

The lists have been made as comprehensive as space will allow but do not include every spelling variation. If a particular variant is not included the following notes may help to ease identification.

All vowel sounds can be considered interchangeable, a,e,i,o,u,y; ph and f; single and double letters, e-ee-ae, f-ff, l-ll, t-tt, m-mm, n-nn, o-oo; a-ah, s-sh, t-th; c-ch-ck-k; s-z; X and Christ. There are also transcription errors to consider, in capitals I,J,L,S,T,Z and in lower case any sequence of i,m,n,r,u,v,w can be difficult to interpret.

Particular regard should be paid to the middle and end of a name as these often contain sounds which are the decisive feature. A list of alternatives should be written down and considered against the variants under each heading. A few days of reflection then usually makes obvious what had seemed so elusive.

For example faced with Bettrys one could be drawn to the Betty/Elizabeth groups but the ending puts it more likely in the Beatrix group. A recent correspondent was faced with a female as Corah, Kerah and Care-happy in three consecutive registers. It will be seen from the indexes that she was probably baptised Kerenhappuch and the variants all arise quite "obviously".

The author welcomes any additions or comments that readers may have.

Acknowledgements

By its very nature this compilation could only have been made by extensive use of existing data and indexes and I would like to express my appreciation for the kindness and effort from many people and in particular the following contributors.

Eddie Blyth, John Dowding, Clive Essery, Graham Fidler, Richard Goring, John Hitchon (Gaelic sources), David Hollick, Rosemary Lockie (analysis of the 1851 census 2% sample), Karen Tayler, John Turner, Dorothy Walker, Martin Whitney.

Bibliography

The coding system used does not claim any necessarily logical connection between variants other than that is what our ancestors have used, right or wrong. The main bibliography tends to concentrate on establishing what the origins were, this comes into its own right when you are dealing with the difficult cases. If the standard codes do not give the solution and you start on a chase of the more obscure diminutive links then it is essential to study the literature. The following I found the most useful.

E.G. Withycombe, *The Oxford Dictionary of English Christian Names*, 3rd Edition, Oxford University Press, 1977. The major work on the etymological origin of names and introduction to the use of first names.

L. Dunkling & W. Gosling, *Dictionary of First Names*, 4th Ed, J.M. Dent 1993. An extensive survey of usage from the 17th to late 20th centuries with diminutives and some etymology.

M. Brown, *The New Book of First Names*, Corgi, 1985. Adds a large number of current names to Withycombe including American and Commonwealth. Some brief etymology and a lot of diminutives.

E.D. Price (editor), *Daily Dispatch, Modern English Dictionary*, Syndicate Publishing Co, London, 1924. A popular picture of names in the 1920's.

D.J. Steel, *National Index of Parish Registers*, Vol. 1, Soc. of Genealogists, 1968. The introductory volume to a series listing the Parish Registers before 1837. A useful chapter on the quirks and variations of first names and how they appear in the Registers.

M.A. Lower, *A Dictionary of Surnames*, Wordsworth Editions, 1988 (reprint of the original published 1860). An earlier work with many references to the interplay of first names and surnames.

C.W. Bardsley, *A Dictionary of English and Welsh Surnames,* London 1901. The definitive work on the origin of surnames with extensive detailed etymology involving first names.

P.H. Reaney, *A Dictionary of British Surnames,* London, 1958. Advancing Bardsley with more recently available material but leaving out large areas of place name origins and other "obvious" origins.

Addresses

Mr A Bardsley, abardsley@iee.org

Roseland, Woodhouse Lane, Gawsworth, Macclesfield, Cheshire, SK11 9QQ, United Kingdom

or

c/o Manchester and Lancashire Family History Society, Clayton House, 59 Piccadilly, Manchester, M1 2AQ

Diminutive	Code	Diminutive	Code	Diminutive	Code	Diminutive	Code
Aannah	ann	Abigill	abi	Adalberta	alb	Aeneas	anu
Aaras	aar	Abijah	aba	Adaline	ada	Aesha	aih
Aaron	aar	Abimelech	abe	Adam	ada	Afra	aph
Ab	abr	Able	abr	Adamina	ada	Agace	aga
Abagail	abi	Abm	abr	Adamus	ada	Agatha	aga
Abagil	abi	Abner	abn	Addelina	ada	Aggie	agn
Abagirl	abi	Abr	abr	Addie	ada	Aggy	agn
Abaigael	abi	Abra	abr	Addison	ada	Agn	agn
Abbelina	app	Abrabham	abr	Addy	ada	Agnas	agn
Abbey	abi	Abrah	abr	Ade	ada	Agnass	agn
Abbie	abi	Abraha	abr	Adekin	ada	Agnes	agn
Abbigal	abi	Abrahaham	abr	Adel	ada	Agness	agn
Abbigale	abi	Abraham	abr	Adela	ada	Agnet	agn
Abbigill	abi	Abrahamina	abr	Adelade	ada	Agneta	agn
Abbot	abb	Abrahem	abr	Adelaid	ada	Agnete	agn
Abby	abi	Abrahim	abr	Adelaide	ada	Agnez	agn
Abbygale	abi	Abram	abr	Adele	ada	Agnis	agn
Abderus	abu	Abreham	abr	Adelia	ada	Agniss	agn
Abdyas	abu	Abrh	abr	Adeliade	ada	Agnus	agn
Abe	abr	Abrham	abr	Adelice	ali	Agnys	agn
Abediah	abu	Abrm	abr	Adelid	ada	Agusta	aug
Abednego	abd	Absalam	abs	Adelide	ada	Agustine	aug
Abednegs	abd	Absalom	abs	Adelie	ada	Agustus	aug
Abegall	abi	Abselon	abs	Adelin	ada	Ahmed	ahm
Abel	abr	Absolam	abs	Adelina	ada	Aibhlin	hel
Abell	abr	Absolan	abs	Adeline	ada	Aida	ada
Abert	alb	Absolom	abs	Adeliza	ali	Aidan	aid
Abey	abi	Absolon	abs	Aden	aid	Aiesha	aih
Abi	abr	Abygall	abi	Aderyn	ade	Aiison	ali
Abia	aba	Acacia	kat	Adhamh	ada	Ailbhe	elv
Abiagail	ahi	Accepted	acc	Adilade	ada	Ailce	ali
Abiah	aba	Ace	ace	Adilinc	ada	Ailean	ala
Abiatha	aba	Acelin	ace	Adin	aid	Aileen	hel
Abiathar	aba	Achile	ach	Adina	adi	Aileson	ali
Abie	abi	Achiles	ach	Adlai	adl	Ailidh	ali
Abiel	aba	Achillas	ach	Admiral	adm	Ailie	ali
Abig	abi	Achille	ach	Adolf	ado	Ailis	ali
Abigah	abi	Achilles	ach	Adolpha	ado	Ailison	ali
Abigaiel	abi	Achim	joc	Adolphe	ado	Ailsa	eli
Abigail	abi	Acie	ace	Adolphus	ado	Ailspit	eli
Abigaile	abi	Ackroyd	ack	Adria	adr	Ailwyn	alw
Abigaill	abi	Ada	ada	Adrian	adr	Aimee	aml
Abigal	abi	Adah	ada	Adriana	adr	Aimie	aml
Abigale	abi	Adaidh	ada	Adrianne	adr	Aina	ann
Abigall	abi	Adaiha	ada	Adriel	adr	Aine	ann
Abigel	abi	Adair	edg	Adrien	adr	Ainsley	ain
Abigial	abi	Adalade	ada	Adriene	adr	Ainthe	ann
Abigiel	abi	Adalaid	ada	Adrienne	adr	Aisha	aih
Abigil	abi	Adalaida	ada	Aed	aid	Aisia	aih
		Adalaide	ada	Aedyline	ada	Aisling	ais

First Names with Codes

Name	Code	Name	Code	Name	Code	Name	Code
Aithne	aid	Alester	ale	Alic	ali	Allyson	ali
Akeroyd	ack	Aleta	alt	Alice	ali	Alma	alm
Al	ala	Aletha	alt	Alicea	ali	Almeina	ame
Alace	ali	Alethea	alt	Alicia	ali	Almena	ame
Alan	ala	Aletta	aet	Aliciae	ali	Almeric	ail
Alanna	ala	Alette	aet	Aliciam	ali	Almina	ame
Alano	ala	Alex	ale	Alicie	ali	Almira	ail
Alanus	ala	Alexa	ale	Alick	alc	Almond	amd
Alaric	alr	Alexader	ale	Alics	ale	Aloisa	aly
Alas	ali	Alexand	ale	Alida	ald	Alonsa	alp
Alasdair	ale	Alexander	ale	Alina	ada	Alonso	alp
Alastair	ale	Alexanderina	ale	Aline	ada	Alowis	aly
Alaxander	ale	Alexanderus	ale	Alis	ali	Aloyisia	aly
Alba	aln	Alexandra	ale	Alisa	ali	Aloysia	aly
Alban	aln	Alexandria	ale	Alisdair	ale	Aloysius	aly
Alber	alb	Alexandrina	ale	Alise	ali	Alperta	alb
Alberic	alc	Alexd	ale	Alisha	ali	Alpheaus	alu
Albert	alb	Alexder	ale	Alisia	ali	Alpheus	alu
Alberta	alb	Alexdr	ale	Alison	ali	Alphoeus	alu
Albertine	alb	Alexeander	ale	Alisone	ali	Alphondo	alp
Albery	aub	Alexia	ale	Alisoun	ali	Alphonsine	alp
Albin	aln	Alexina	ale	Alistair	ale	Alphonso	alp
Albina	aln	Alexine	ale	Alister	ale	Alpin	apl
Albinia	aln	Alexis	ale	Alithea	alt	Alpine	apl
Albion	aln	Alexr	ale	Alixander	ale	Alse	ali
Albright	alb	Alexsander	ale	Allan	ala	Alsie	ali
Alby	elv	Alexssaunder	ale	Allane	ala	Althea	alt
Alce	ali	Aley	ali	Allas	ali	Alucia	ali
Alcina	aci	Aleyn	ala	Allaster	ale	Alured	alf
Alda	ald	Alf	alf	Allen	ala	Alva	aln
Alden	alw	Alfd	alf	Alles	ali	Alvah	aln
Aldhelm	alh	Alfie	alf	Alleson	ali	Alvan	alw
Aldo	ald	Alfonce	alp	Allesona	ali	Alvar	alv
Aldous	ald	Alfonso	alp	Alless	ali	Alvarah	alv
Aldred	ald	Alford	alf	Allex	ale	Alvedine	avl
Aldreda	ald	Alfrd	alf	Allexander	ale	Alven	alw
Aldwin	alw	Alfread	alf	Allexr	ale	Alvena	alw
Aldwyn	alw	Alfred	alf	Alley	ali	Alverdine	avl
Alec	ale	Alfreda	alf	Allfred	alf	Alverna	alw
Aled	ael	Alfredo	alf	Alli	ale	Alvery	alf
Aleen	ala	Alfrid	alf	Allice	ali	Alvin	alw
Aleine	ala	Alfried	alf	Allick	ale	Alvina	alw
Alen	ala	Alga	agl	Allie	ali	Alvira	alw
Alena	mad	Algar	agl	Allin	ala	Alvy	elv
Alene	mad	Alger	agl	Allis	ali	Alwyn	alw
Ales	ali	Algernon	alg	Allison	ali	Alwyna	alw
Alese	ali	Algie	alg	Allon	alo	Alxr	ale
Aleson	ali	Algy	alg	Allse	ali	Aly	ali
Alessone	ali	Ali	ali	Allwood	all	Alyce	ali
Alessoun	ali	Alias	ali	Ally	ali	Alyn	ala

Name	Code	Name	Code	Name	Code	Name	Code
Alys	ali	Amor	amu	Andr	and	Anna	ann
Alysia	ali	Amorous	amu	Andra	and	Annabel	aml
Am	aml	Amos	amo	Andraw	and	Annabell	aml
Ama	aml	Amose	amo	Andraye	and	Annabella	aml
Amabel	aml	Amoss	amo	Andrea	and	Annae	ann
Amable	aml	Amphelice	phy	Andreana	and	Annah	ann
Amalia	emm	Amphelicia	phy	Andreas	and	Annais	agn
Aman	ama	Amphelisia	phy	Andrette	and	Annalie	aen
Amand	ama	Amphillis	phy	Andreu	and	Annalisa	aen
Amanda	ama	Amphlis	phy	Andrew	and	Annaple	aml
Amariah	amh	Amphliss	phy	Andrewe	and	Annas	agn
Amaris	amh	Amphyllis	phy	Andrewina	and	Anndra	and
Amaryllis	amr	Amplena	phy	Andria	and	Anne	ann
Amas	aml	Amples	phy	Andrienne	and	Anneka	ann
Amata	aml	Amplias	phy	Andrietta	and	Annelie	aen
Amber	abm	Amplis	phy	Andrina	and	Anneliese	aen
Ambler	abm	Ampliss	phy	Andro	and	Annes	agn
Ambrese	amb	Amry	aml	Androe	and	Annetta	ann
Ambros	amb	Amus	amo	Androu	and	Annette	ann
Ambrose	amb	Amy	aml	Androw	and	Anney	ann
Ambrosina	amb	Amyas	aml	Androwe	and	Annice	agn
Ambrosse	amb	An	ann	Andw	and	Annie	ann
Ambrus	amb	Ana	ann	Andy	and	Annika	ann
Amchia	ami	Anabella	aml	Ane	ann	Annis	agn
Ame	aml	Anae	ann	Aneira	ane	Anniss	agn
Amee	aml	Anaebella	aml	Aneirin	ane	Annissa	agn
Amelia	emm	Anagusta	aug	Anes	agn	Annita	ann
Amelinda	emm	Anah	ann	Anese	agn	Annora	hel
Ameline	emm	Anas	agn	Anetta	ann	Annot	agn
Amellia	emm	Anastasia	ana	Aneurin	ane	Anny	ann
Amer	aml	Anastatia	ana	Angel	ang	Annys	agn
Amey	aml	Ancel	ans	Angela	ang	Anocea	non
Amfelice	phy	Ancelm	ans	Angelica	ang	Anona	non
Amia	aml	Ancelot	lan	Angelina	ang	Ansell	ans
Amiable	aml	Anchetil	ask	Angelo	ang	Anselm	ans
Amias	aml	Anchitel	ask	Angharad	anc	Anselma	ans
Amica	ami	Anchor	anc	Angie	ang	Ansketil	ask
Amice	ami	Anchoret	anc	Angle	ang	Anskettell	ask
Amie	aml	Anchoretta	anc	Angnes	agn	Ansley	ain
Amies	aml	Ancilla	ans	Angus	anu	Anslow	ano
Amilia	emm	Ancrait	anc	Angusina	anu	Anstes	ana
Amina	wil	Ancras	anc	Angy	ang	Anstey	ana
Aminadab	wil	Ancret	anc	Anice	agn	Anstice	ana
Aminah	wil	Ancreta	anc	Anika	ann	Anstis	ana
Aminta	amn	And	and	Anis	agn	Anstiss	ana
Amis	aml	Andera	and	Anise	agn	Anth	ant
Amley	emm	Anderina	and	Anita	ann	Anthea	ant
Ammy	emm	Anders	and	Anketil	ask	Anthi	ant
Amo	amo	Anderson	and	Anketin	ask	Anthoinus	ant
Amophless	phy	Anderston	and	Ann	ann	Anthoney	ant

First Names with Codes

Name	Code	Name	Code	Name	Code	Name	Code
Anthonie	ant	Archy	arc	Artie	art	Auguste	aug
Anthonies	ant	Arelia	aur	Artina	art	Augustin	aug
Anthonij	ant	Areta	ara	Artis	art	Augustine	aug
Anthony	ant	Aretas	ara	Artisidilla	art	Augustins	aug
Anthonye	ant	Aretha	ara	Arty	art	Augustinus	aug
Anthoy	ant	Argate	arg	Aruther	art	Augustus	aug
Antione	ant	Argent	arg	Asa	asa	Auley	ola
Antjuan	ant	Ariadne	ari	Ascelina	ace	Aurea	aur
Antoinette	ant	Ariane	ari	Aselma	ans	Aurelia	aur
Anton	ant	Arleen	air	Asenath	ase	Aurelian	aur
Antone	ant	Arlene	air	Ash	ash	Aureole	aur
Antoney	ant	Arletta	cha	Asher	asr	Auriel	aur
Antoni	ant	Arlette	cha	Ashey	ash	Aurora	ori
Antonia	ant	Arley	arl	Ashlea	ash	Aurther	art
Antonie	ant	Arline	air	Ashlee	ash	Aurthur	art
Antonius	ant	Arlyne	air	Ashleigh	ash	Austen	aug
Antony	ant	Armand	hem	Ashley	ash	Austin	aug
Antuan	ant	Armando	hem	Ashlie	ash	Austine	aug
Antwan	ant	Armigil	erm	Ashling	ais	Austis	aug
Anwen	anw	Armin	hem	Ashton	aso	Auston	aug
Anwyl	aml	Armina	hem	Ashwell	ash	Austyn	aug
Anwyn	anw	Arminda	hem	Asketh	ase	Auther	art
Anya	ann	Arminel	hem	Asketil	ask	Author	art
Aodh	hug	Arnaud	arn	Aspasia	asp	Authur	art
Aonghas	anu	Arnie	arn	Asta	ast	Ava	avi
Aphra	aph	Arnold	arn	Astley	ash	Avaril	ave
Applina	app	Arnoldine	arn	Aston	aso	Aveas	avi
Appoline	app	Arnot	arn	Astrid	ast	Aveline	eve
Appollo	app	Arnott	arn	Atalanta	ata	Avenel	eve
Appolonia	app	Aron	aar	Athalia	atl	Averhilda	ave
April	ave	Arrabella	aml	Athanasius	atn	Averil	ave
Aquila	aqu	Arraminta	amn	Athanye	atn	Averilda	ave
Arabel	aml	Arran	aar	Athelia	atl	Avery	alf
Arabella	aml	Arron	aar	Athelstan	ath	Aves	avi
Araminta	amn	Arskein	ers	Athene	ate	Avice	avi
Araunah	aru	Arskine	ers	Ather	art	Avis	avi
Arban	urb	Art	art	Athol	ato	Avisa	avi
Arbuthnot	ant	Artair	art	Athur	art	Avner	abn
Arch	arc	Artemas	are	Atkinson	atk	Awdrie	eth
Archabald	arc	Artemisia	are	Auberon	aub	Ayesha	aih
Archbald	arc	Arter	art	Aubert	alb	Ayleen	ala
Archbd	arc	Arterei	art	Aubrey	aub	Ayles	ali
Archbold	arc	Arthene	art	Aubry	aub	Aylmer	elm
Archd	arc	Arther	art	Audie	eth	Aylwin	alw
Archelaus	her	Arthour	art	Audrey	eth	Azalea	azl
Archer	arc	Arthur	art	Augnes	agn	Azariah	aza
Archibald	arc	Arthure	art	Augstin	aug	Azenath	ase
Archiball	arc	Arthuretta	art	August	aug	Azubah	azu
Archibold	arc	Arthuri	art	Augusta	aug	Bab	bar
Archie	arc	Arthurina	art	Augustas	aug	Babbie	bar

Name	Code	Name	Code	Name	Code	Name	Code
Babette	eli	Barrie	bay	Beatty	bea	Benn	ben
Babs	bar	Barrington	bia	Beau	bae	Bennet	bee
Baden	bda	Barron	bna	Beaumont	bae	Bennett	bee
Bagshaw	bag	Barry	bay	Becca	reb	Bennie	ben
Bailey	bai	Barrymore	bam	Beccy	reb	Benny	ben
Baker	bka	Bart	bat	Beck	reb	Benoni	beo
Bal	bab	Barthol	bat	Becky	reb	Benson	bne
Bala	bab	Bartholemew	bat	Bede	bed	Bentley	bnt
Baldie	arc	Bartholmew	bat	Bedelia	brd	Berengaria	beg
Baldric	bad	Bartholmewe	bat	Bedford	bef	Berenger	beg
Baldwin	bal	Bartholomew	bat	Bee	bea	Berenice	bei
Balthasar	baa	Bartholomewe	bat	Belinda	bel	Berenthia	bih
Bamber	bma	Barthw	bat	Bell	eli	Beresford	brf
Banjamin	ben	Bartie	alb	Bella	eli	Berihert	ben
Banjan	ben	Bartle	bat	Bellah	eli	Berkeley	bek
Banks	bak	Bartlet	bat	Belle	eli	Bernadette	ber
Baptist	bap	Barton	bto	Bemjamin	ben	Bernadine	ber
Baptista	bap	Bartram	bem	Ben	ben	Bernal	bnr
Barabal	bar	Baruch	bau	Benedict	bee	Bernard	ber
Barbar	bar	Barzilla	baz	Benedicta	bee	Bernet	ber
Barbara	bar	Barzillai	baz	Benejaman	ben	Bernhard	ber
Barbarah	bar	Basil	bas	Benezer	ebe	Bernice	bei
Barbaraye	bar	Basilia	bas	Bengaman	ben	Bernie	bei
Barbarie	bar	Basilla	bas	Bengamin	ben	Berresford	brf
Barbaro	bar	Bassett	bsa	Bengeman	ben	Berry	bei
Barbarra	bar	Bassil	bas	Bengn	ben	Bersaba	bah
Barbary	bar	Bastian	seb	Beniamin	ben	Bert	alb
Barber	bar	Bat	bat	Beniamini	ben	Berta	bet
Barbera	bar	Batheanna	eli	Benita	bee	Bertha	bet
Barbery	bar	Bathia	eli	Benj	ben	Berther	bet
Barberye	bar	Bathsheba	bah	Benja	ben	Berthia	bet
Barbie	bar	Bathshua	bah	Benjaby	ben	Berthold	bch
Barbra	bar	Bathurst	bat	Benjam	ben	Bertholemi	bat
Barby	bar	Bathya	eli	Benjaman	ben	Bertie	alb
Barclay	bek	Batson	bat	Benjamen	ben	Bertina	alb
Bardolph	bao	Batty	bat	Benjamie	ben	Bertram	bcm
Barker	bkr	Baubie	bar	Benjamin	ben	Bertrand	bem
Barnabas	ban	Baudrey	bad	Benjamine	ben	Berwyn	bew
Barnabus	ban	Bayne	bya	Benjamn	ben	Beryl	bey
Barnaby	ban	Bazil	bas	Benjamon	ben	Besey	eli
Barnard	ber	Bead	bde	Benje	ben	Bess	eli
Barne	ban	Beat	bea	Benjeman	ben	Besse	eli
Barnel	bnr	Beata	bea	Benjiaman	ben	Bessey	eli
Barnes	brs	Beathag	eli	Benjiman	ben	Bessie	eli
Barnet	ber	Beathea	eli	Benjimin	ben	Bessy	eli
Barnett	ber	Beaton	bea	Benjm	ben	Bet	eli
Barney	ban	Beatria	bea	Benjman	ben	Beta	eli
Barny	ban	Beatrice	bea	Benjmin	ben	Betey	eli
Baron	bna	Beatrices	bea	Benjmn	ben	Beth	eli
Barrett	bte	Beatrix	bea	Benjn	ben	Betha	eli

First Names with Codes

Name	Code	Name	Code	Name	Code	Name	Code
Bethan	bth	Billyanna	wil	Bonny	boi	Britannia	brt
Bethany	bth	Bina	sab	Booth	boo	Britney	brt
Bethea	eli	Binah	sab	Boris	bor	Britt	brd
Betheah	eli	Bingamin	ben	Boswell	bos	Brittan	brt
Bethel	eli	Biniamen	ben	Bowman	bow	Brittany	brt
Bethenia	eli	Binns	bin	Boy	boy	Brock	brk
Bethia	eli	Birch	bic	Boyce	boe	Broderick	brr
Bethiah	eli	Birdie	bir	Boyd	byo	Brodie	bod
Bethie	eli	Birt	alb	Brad	bra	Bronwen	bro
Bethsheba	bah	Birtha	bet	Bradley	bra	Brook	brk
Bethune	bth	Birtie	alb	Bradshaw	brh	Brooke	brk
Betina	eli	Birty	alb	Brain	bri	Brooksbank	brk
Betrice	bea	Bithia	eli	Bram	abr	Brown	brw
Betriche	bea	Bithiah	eli	Bramley	abr	Bruce	bru
Betrix	bea	Bitty	eli	Bramwell	brm	Brunhild	brn
Betsay	eli	Blackburn	blc	Branden	bre	Bruno	bun
Betsee	eli	Blaine	bli	Brandon	bre	Brya	bri
Betsey	eli	Blair	blr	Branwell	brm	Bryan	bri
Betsie	eli	Blaise	bls	Branwen	bro	Bryce	brc
Betsy	eli	Blake	blk	Breedon	bre	Bryden	byd
Bett	eli	Blanch	bla	Bregit	brd	Bryn	bry
Bette	eli	Blanche	bla	Brenainn	bre	Brynly	bry
Betteras	bea	Blanchiam	bla	Brenda	bre	Brynmor	bry
Betteria	eli	Blase	bls	Brendan	bre	Bryon	bri
Betterice	bea	Blauncha	bla	Brenden	bre	Bud	bud
Bettey	eli	Blenda	bre	Brent	btn	Buddy	bud
Bettie	eli	Bleyana	wil	Brett	btr	Bunny	bei
Bettina	eli	Blihanna	wil	Brewster	bwr	Bunty	but
Bettrice	bea	Blinnie	bla	Brian	bri	Burnard	ber
Bettrys	bea	Blith	bly	Briana	bri	Burnet	bur
Bettsey	eli	Blithman	bly	Brianus	bri	Burnitt	bur
Bettsy	eli	Blodwen	blo	Brice	brc	Burrill	bey
Betty	eli	Blodwyn	blo	Bride	brd	Burt	alb
Bety	eli	Blossom	blm	Bridger	brd	Burton	alb
Beula	beu	Bluebell	blu	Bridget	brd	Butler	bul
Beulah	beu	Blyth	bly	Bridgett	brd	By	eli
Bev	bev	Blythe	bly	Bridgget	brd	Byron	byr
Bevan	bve	Blythman	bly	Bridgit	brd	Bythia	eli
Beverley	bev	Boadicea	boc	Bridgitt	brd	Cacia	kat
Bevin	bve	Boaz	boz	Brigdet	brd	Caddie	cao
Bevis	bes	Bob	rob	Briget	brd	Cadelia	cao
Bianca	bla	Bobbie	rob	Brigett	brd	Cadell	cda
Bibby	viv	Bobby	rob	Brigham	brg	Cadwalladar	cad
Bibiana	viv	Bolton	bol	Brigid	brd	Cadwalleder	cad
Biddie	brd	Bonabel	boi	Brigit	brd	Caecile	cec
Biddy	brd	Bonamy	bon	Brigitta	brd	Caesar	caa
Bidy	brd	Bonar	bno	Brilliana	brl	Caezer	caa
Bill	wil	Bonaventure	boa	Brinley	bil	Cahrles	cha
Billie	wil	Bonita	boi	Briony	bri	Cai	kat
Billy	wil	Bonnie	boi	Britania	brt	Cailean	nic

Name	Code	Name	Code	Name	Code	Name	Code
Cain	kan	Carleton	crn	Cassius	cas	Catren	kat
Caine	kan	Carley	cha	Cassy	cas	Catrin	kat
Caio	gai	Carlie	cha	Caster	cas	Catrina	kat
Cairistiona	chr	Carlin	cao	Castle	csa	Catrine	kat
Caitlin	kat	Carline	cao	Catarina	kat	Catriona	kat
Caius	gai	Carlo	cha	Catarine	kat	Catron	kat
Calab	cal	Carloine	cao	Cataryne	kat	Caw	gai
Calam	clu	Carlos	cha	Cate	kat	Ceaser	caa
Caleb	cal	Carlotta	cha	Cater	cta	Cecelia	cec
Caleby	cal	Carlton	crn	Caterane	kat	Cecil	cec
Caleh	cal	Carly	cha	Caterena	kat	Cecila	cec
Call	cal	Carlyn	cao	Caterina	kat	Cecile	cec
Callum	clu	Carmel	cae	Caterine	kat	Ceciley	cec
Calob	cal	Carmen	cae	Catern	kat	Cecilia	cec
Calorine	cao	Caro	cao	Cath	kat	Cecilie	cec
Calum	clu	Carol	cao	Cathaream	kat	Cecill	cec
Calvert	cat	Carola	cao	Catharen	kat	Cecily	cec
Calvin	kel	Carole	cao	Catharin	kat	Ceclia	cec
Cam	cam	Carolin	cao	Catharine	kat	Cedric	ced
Camelia	cam	Carolina	cao	Cathbert	cut	Cedrych	ced
Cameron	cma	Caroline	cao	Cathe	kat	Ceinwen	cei
Camilla	cam	Carolyn	cao	Cather	kat	Ceit	kat
Cammie	cam	Caron	kee	Catheraine	kat	Celena	cel
Cammy	cam	Carr	cao	Catheran	kat	Celeste	cel
Campbell	cab	Carraline	cao	Cathereine	kat	Celestine	cel
Candace	can	Carren	kee	Catheren	kat	Celia	cec
Candes	can	Carrie	cao	Catherena	kat	Celina	cel
Candia	can	Carrilion	cao	Catherin	kat	Cephas	cep
Candice	can	Carrin	kee	Catherina	kat	Cerdic	car
Candida	can	Carrisa	car	Catherine	kat	Ceredig	car
Candy	can	Carrol	cao	Catherinr	kat	Ceridwen	cer
Captain	cap	Carroline	cao	Cathern	kat	Ceris	cey
Car	kee	Carron	kce	Catherne	kat	Cerris	cey
Cara	car	Carry	cao	Catheryne	kat	Cerys	cey
Caradoc	car	Carson	crs	Cathiriene	kat	Cesar	caa
Caradog	car	Carter	crr	Cathirine	kat	Ceselia	cec
Caraline	cao	Cartharine	kat	Cathleen	kat	Chad	chd
Caralyn	cao	Cary	cao	Cathn	kat	Chaim	hym
Carden	cod	Caryl	cao	Cathne	kat	Chales	cha
Cardwalader	cad	Caryn	kee	Cathorine	kat	Challotte	cha
Caren	kee	Carys	car	Cathr	kat	Chalotte	cha
Carew	kat	Casandra	cas	Cathrain	kat	Chalrotte	cha
Carey	cha	Casey	cas	Cathraine	kat	Champion	chm
Cariline	cao	Casimir	csi	Cathrane	kat	Chandra	chn
Carin	kee	Casper	jap	Cathrein	kat	Chantal	cht
Carina	car	Cass	cas	Cathren	kat	Chapel	cah
Carita	car	Cassandra	cas	Cathrin	kat	Chapman	chp
Carl	cha	Cassey	cas	Cathrine	kat	Chappell	cah
Carla	cha	Cassia	cas	Cathy	kat	Char	cha
Carlene	cao	Cassie	cas	Catie	kat	Chares	cha

Name	Code	Name	Code	Name	Code	Name	Code
Charis	car	Chisthopher	chr	Christopheri	chr	Clarance	cla
Charitie	car	Chloe	che	Christopherus	chr	Clare	cla
Charity	car	Chls	cha	Christophr	chr	Clarence	cla
Charl	cha	Chr	chr	Christor	chr	Clari	cla
Charlene	cha	Chrestane	chr	Christouer	chr	Claribel	cla
Charles	cha	Chris	chr	Christr	chr	Clarice	cla
Charlesworth	cha	Chrisandra	chr	Christy	chr	Claricy	cla
Charlet	cha	Chrispin	cri	Christyan	chr	Clarimente	clr
Charlett	cha	Chrisr	chr	Christyfer	chr	Clarimond	clr
Charlette	cha	Chrissie	chr	Chrles	cha	Clarinda	cla
Charley	cha	Chrisstopher	chr	Chrus	chr	Clarindo	cla
Charlie	cha	Christ	chr	Chrysogon	chy	Clarissa	cla
Charline	cha	Christabel	chr	Chs	cha	Clarissia	cla
Charlis	cha	Christabell	chr	Chuck	cha	Clark	clk
Charllote	cha	Christabella	chr	Chursty	chr	Clarke	clk
Charllotta	cha	Christain	chr	Ciara	kie	Clarrie	cla
Charllotte	cha	Christaine	chr	Cibill	sib	Clarry	cla
Charloote	cha	Christan	chr	Cicel	cec	Claud	cld
Charlot	cha	Christana	chr	Ciceley	cec	Claude	cld
Charlote	cha	Christane	chr	Cicelia	cec	Claudeen	cld
Charlotee	cha	Christann	chr	Cicelie	cec	Claudelle	cld
Charlott	cha	Christanna	chr	Cicely	cec	Claudette	cld
Charlotta	cha	Christean	chr	Cicial	cec	Claudia	cld
Charlotte	cha	Christeane	chr	Cicil	cec	Claudina	cld
Charlottee	cha	Christen	chr	Cicile	cec	Claudine	cld
Charls	cha	Christena	chr	Cicilia	cec	Claughton	cld
Charlton	cho	Christephir	chr	Cicilie	cec	Clay	cly
Charmaine	cae	Christian	chr	Cicill	cec	Clayton	cly
Charmian	cae	Christiana	chr	Cicily	cec	Clea	clp
Charolette	cha	Christianah	chr	Ciliscia	cec	Cleem	cle
Charoline	cao	Christiane	chr	Cilla	prs	Clem	cle
Chars	cha	Christianna	chr	Cimmie	cyn	Clemence	cle
Chas	cha	Christibella	chr	Cindinia	luc	Clemency	cle
Chatherine	kat	Christie	chr	Cindy	luc	Clemens	cle
Chatty	cha	Christien	chr	Ciorstaidh	chr	Clement	cle
Chauncy	chu	Christin	chr	Ciprian	cyp	Clementia	cle
Chavon	joa	Christina	chr	Cirstane	chr	Clementina	cle
Chay	cha	Christine	chr	Cirstin	chr	Clementine	cle
Chedham	chh	Christinia	chr	Cirsty	chr	Clemina	cle
Cheetham	chh	Christmas	chs	Ciselia	cec	Clemmey	cle
Chelsea	chl	Christn	chr	Cislea	cec	Clemmie	cle
Chere	cha	Christo	chr	Cisley	cec	Cleo	clp
Cherie	car	Christofer	chr	Ciss	cec	Cleopatra	clp
Cherry	car	Christoferus	chr	Cissy	cec	Cleophas	clp
Cheryl	cha	Christoffer	chr	Claira	cla	Cleris	cla
Chester	ceh	Christon	chr	Claire	cla	Clerk	clk
Chet	ceh	Christoper	chr	Clancy	clc	Cliff	cli
Chick	cha	Christoph	chr	Clara	cla	Clifford	cli
Chirstian	chr	Christophe	chr	Clarabelle	cla	Clifton	cli
Chirsty	chr	Christopher	chr	Clarah	cla	Clint	cln

Name	Code	Name	Code	Name	Code	Name	Code
Clinton	cln	Constant	cos	Cowper	cop	Cuthbt	cut
Clive	clv	Constanten	cos	Craig	cra	Cuthbte	cut
Clodagh	clo	Constantia	cos	Craven	crv	Cutherbert	cut
Cloe	che	Constantina	cos	Crawford	crw	Cuthr	cut
Clorinda	cla	Constantine	cos	Creighton	crg	Cybil	sib
Clotilda	clt	Constartia	cos	Cressida	cre	Cydney	sid
Coinneach	ken	Constophia	cos	Cresswell	ces	Cynthia	cyn
Colan	nic	Constophia	cos	Cressy	cre	Cyprian	cyp
Cole	clm	Consuelo	cos	Crighton	crg	Cyriack	cyi
Coleen	nic	Conway	cow	Crispian	cri	Cyril	cyr
Coleman	clm	Cook	cok	Crispin	cri	Cyrilla	cyr
Colen	nic	Cooper	cop	Crispiny	cri	Cyrus	cyu
Coleridge	cog	Cora	cor	Crisscy	chr	Daborah	deb
Colet	nic	Corabelle	cor	Crissie	chr	Dacian	dac
Colette	nic	Corah	kee	Crissy	chr	Dadie	dei
Coley	clm	Coral	cor	Cristaine	chr	Daemon	dam
Colin	nic	Corale	cor	Cristan	chr	Daff	dap
Colina	nic	Coralie	cor	Cristane	chr	Daffie	dap
Colleen	nic	Coraline	cor	Cristian	chr	Daffyd	dav
Collen	nic	Coranea	cor	Cristiana	chr	Dagmar	dag
Collette	nic	Corben	cbo	Cristiane	chr	Dahlia	dah
Colley	coy	Corbett	cob	Cristin	chr	Dai	dav
Collin	nic	Corbin	cbo	Cristina	chr	Daibhidh	dav
Collingwood	coi	Cordelia	cod	Cristofer	chr	Daiel	dan
Collis	coy	Cordie	cod	Criston	chr	Daisey	mar
Colm	clm	Coretta	cor	Cristopher	chr	Daisie	mar
Colman	clm	Corina	cor	Cristover	chr	Daisy	mar
Colonel	cno	Corinna	cor	Critchlow	crt	Daived	dav
Colston	cot	Corinne	cor	Crofton	crf	Dal	dal
Colum	clu	Corisande	cro	Crompton	crm	Dale	dal
Columba	clu	Corleana	crl	Crosby	crb	Daley	dla
Columbina	clu	Corneilus	coe	Crowther	crh	Dalia	dah
Columbine	clu	Cornelia	coe	Crustian	chr	Dallas	das
Colville	cov	Cornelias	coe	Crustina	chr	Dalmen	dam
Colvin	cvo	Cornelious	coe	Crystal	chr	Dalton	dat
Comfort	com	Cornelius	coe	Cudbart	cut	Daly	dla
Comforta	com	Cornellius	coe	Cudberde	cut	Damaris	daa
Con	cos	Corneluis	coe	Cudbert	cut	Damen	dam
Conal	col	Cornenilius	coe	Cuddie	cut	Dameris	daa
Conan	con	Cornes	coe	Cuddy	cut	Damian	dam
Conn	cos	Cornie	coe	Cullam	clu	Damon	dam
Connant	con	Cornwallis	cnw	Curnialus	coe	Damris	daa
Connell	col	Coroline	cor	Curt	cou	Dan	dan
Connie	cos	Correen	cor	Curtis	cur	Dana	dan
Connor	cos	Corry	cor	Cutbard	cut	Danal	dan
Conrad	coa	Cosmo	coo	Cutberd	cut	Dandy	and
Conroy	cnr	Costin	cos	Cutbert	cut	Dane	dan
Constance	cos	Coulson	nic	Cuth	cut	Daneal	dan
Constancy	cos	Coulton	nic	Cuthbert	cut	Daneen	dan
Constanie	cos	Courtenay	cou	Cuthbertus	cut	Danel	dan
		Courtney	cou				

First Names with Codes

Danella	dan	Darius	dra	Dede	dei	Derenda	der
Danette	dan	Darleen	day	Dee	eth	Deric	der
Dani	dan	Darlene	day	Deena	din	Dermod	deo
Danial	dan	Darley	day	Deidra	dei	Dermot	deo
Danice	dan	Daron	dae	Deidre	dei	Derreck	der
Daniel	dan	Darrell	day	Deidrie	dei	Derrick	der
Daniele	dan	Darren	dae	Deiniol	dan	Derrie	der
Daniell	dan	Darryl	day	Deinol	dan	Derry	der
Daniella	dan	Daryl	day	Deio	dav	Deryck	der
Danielle	dan	Daryn	dae	Deirdre	dei	Des	dem
Danielus	dan	Dasey	mar	Del	del	Desdemona	ded
Danil	dan	Dasi	mar	Delia	del	Desiderata	des
Danile	dan	Dasie	mar	Deliah	del	Desire	des
Danill	dan	Dathi	dav	Delice	dle	Desiree	des
Danise	dan	Dav	dav	Delicia	dle	Desmond	dem
Danita	dan	Davd	dav	Delila	del	Devany	dav
Danl	dan	Dave	dav	Delilah	del	Devina	dav
Danll	dan	Davet	dav	Delise	dle	Devorah	deb
Dann	dan	Davey	dav	Della	del	Devra	deb
Danna	dan	David	dav	Delmar	dea	Dewey	dav
Danne	dan	Davide	dav	Delores	dol	Dewi	dav
Danneall	dan	Davidi	dav	Delphi	dep	Dexter	dex
Danniel	dan	Davidina	dav	Delphine	dep	Di	din
Danniell	dan	Davie	dav	Delphus	ado	Diamond	dia
Danny	dan	Davied	dav	Delsie	dul	Diana	din
Dansea	dan	Davin	dav	Delta	det	Dianah	din
Dansey	dan	Davina	dav	Demas	daa	Diane	din
Dansy	dan	Davinia	dav	Den	den	Dianiah	din
Dante	dur	Davis	dav	Dena	din	Dianna	din
Danuel	dan	Davit	dav	Denes	den	Diannah	din
Danya	dan	Davy	dav	Denham	deh	Dianne	din
Danyele	dan	Daw	dav	Denice	den	Diarmuid	deo
Danyell	dan	Dawn	daw	Denies	den	Dick	ric
Danzie	dan	Dawsabell	dul	Denis	den	Dickinson	ric
Danzy	dan	Dawson	dav	Denise	den	Dickon	ric
Daphne	dap	Day	dav	Deniss	den	Dierdrie	dei
Daphny	dap	Dean	dne	Denness	den	Digby	dig
Dar	dra	Deana	din	Dennet	den	Diggory	dio
Dara	dra	Deanna	din	Denney	den	Dille	dil
Darah	dra	Deanne	din	Dennis	den	Dillian	dyl
Daran	dae	Deb	deb	Dennison	den	Dillon	dyl
Daratie	dra	Debbie	deb	Denny	den	Dilys	dil
Darby	deo	Debora	deb	Dennys	den	Dina	din
Darcey	dar	Deborah	deb	Dent	dnt	Dinah	din
Darcy	dar	Deborough	deb	Denton	dnt	Dinas	den
Darell	day	Deborrah	deb	Denver	dev	Dinis	den
Daren	dae	Debra	deb	Denys	den	Dinnah	din
Daria	dra	Debrah	deb	Denzil	dez	Dinnis	den
Darias	dra	Decima	dec	Derby	deo	Diogenes	den
Darie	dra	Decimus	dec	Derek	der	Diones	den

Name	Code	Name	Code	Name	Code	Name	Code
Dionis	den	Donovan	doo	Dorotiae	dor	Dughall	dou
Dionisius	den	Dora	dor	Dorrathy	dor	Dughlas	dou
Dionne	den	Dorah	dor	Dorretey	dor	Dukana	mam
Dionys	den	Dorate	dor	Dorrien	doe	Duke	mam
Dionysia	den	Dorath	dor	Dorrit	dor	Dulce	dul
Dionysius	den	Doratha	dor	Dorrothy	dor	Dulcibel	dul
Diorbhail	dor	Dorathea	dor	Dorthea	dor	Dulcibella	dul
Diot	den	Dorathee	dor	Dorthy	dor	Dulcie	dul
Dirk	der	Dorathie	dor	Dory	isi	Dulsebe	dul
Divarus	div	Dorathy	dor	Dorythe	dor	Dulsebella	dul
Divers	div	Doratie	dor	Dorytye	dor	Dulsie	dul
Diverus	div	Dorca	doc	Dot	dor	Dump	hum
Divcs	div	Dorcas	doc	Dothy	dor	Dumphry	hum
Divina	dav	Dorcase	doc	Dotty	dor	Dun	dun
Dixon	ric	Dorcus	doc	Doug	dou	Duncan	dun
Dob	rob	Dore	isi	Dougal	dou	Dunstan	dus
Doctor	dco	Doreen	doe	Dougald	dou	Durand	dur
Dod	geo	Doreley	dor	Dougall	dou	Durante	dur
Dodge	rog	Dorena	doe	Douglas	dou	Dvd	dav
Dodie	dor	Dorene	doe	Douglass	dou	Dwain	dwa
Dodo	dor	Dorete	dor	Dousabell	dul	Dwaine	dwa
Doileag	don	Doretha	dor	Dow	dul	Dwayne	dwa
Doirean	doe	Dorethe	dor	Dowe	dul	Dwight	dwi
Dolena	dor	Dorethy	dor	Downs	dow	Dyer	dye
Dolf	ado	Doria	doe	Dowsabel	dul	Dylan	dyl
Dolina	dor	Dorian	doe	Dowse	dul	Dyllis	dil
Doll	dor	Dorice	dor	Dowsland	dul	Dylus	dil
Dolley	dor	Dorinda	doe	Doyle	dou	Dymoke	dyo
Dolly	dor	Doris	dor	Dreena	and	Dymphna	dym
Dolores	dol	Doritha	dor	Drena	and	Dympna	dym
Dolphus	ado	Dorithe	dor	Drew	dro	Dynas	den
Domhnall	dan	Dorithie	dor	Drewsila	dru	Dyonis	den
Dominic	dom	Dorithy	dor	Drina	and	Dyonisius	den
Dominica	dom	Dorithye	dor	Drogo	dro	Dysnysius	den
Dominick	dom	Doritie	dor	Drucella	dru	Dyson	den
Dominy	dom	Dority	dor	Drucilla	dru	Dysory	des
Domnick	dom	Doritye	dor	Drummond	drm	Eachann	hec
Don	don	Dorkis	doc	Drumond	drm	Eachdoin	hec
Donal	don	Doroothy	dor	Druscilla	dru	Eacy	est
Donald	don	Doroth	dor	Drusila	dru	Eadie	edw
Donavon	doo	Dorotha	dor	Drusilla	dru	Eairdsidh	arc
Dond	don	Dorothe	dor	Drusylla	dru	Ealasaid	eli
Donella	don	Dorothea	dor	Dthy	dor	Ealoner	hel
Dong	dou	Dorotheam	dor	Duane	dwa	Eame	edw
Donkin	don	Dorothee	dor	Dudley	dud	Eamon	edw
Donna	dom	Dorothey	dor	Duene	due	Ean	joh
Donnchadh	dun	Dorothia	dor	Dug	dou	Eardley	ead
Donnella	don	Dorothiae	dor	Dugal	dou	Earl	ear
Donnet	dot	Dorothie	dor	Dugald	dou	Earlene	ear
Donnie	don	Dorothy	dor	Dugd	dou	Earnest	ern

Name	Code	Name	Code	Name	Code	Name	Code
Earnshaw	ean	Edom	ada	Eion	joh	Eleoner	hel
Earth	eat	Edony	ido	Eira	eir	Eleonor	hel
Eartha	eat	Edred	edr	Eireen	ire	Eleonora	hel
Earthur	art	Edric	edi	Eirene	ire	Eleonore	hel
Easter	est	Edrice	edi	Eithne	ann	Elesabeth	eli
Easther	est	Edrus	edi	Eithrig	eup	Elesbeth	eli
Ebbaneza	ebe	Eduardi	edw	Eiz	eli	Elesebeth	eli
Eben	ebe	Eduardus	edw	Eiza	eli	Elcsha	eli
Ebeneer	ebe	Edvardi	edw	Eizabeth	eli	Elespet	eli
Ebenesar	ebe	Edvardus	edw	Eizabth	eli	Elexius	ale
Ebeneser	ebe	Edvy	edw	Ekin	eki	Elezabath	eli
Ebenezar	ebe	Edw	edw	El	hel	Elezabeth	eli
Ebenezer	ebe	Edward	edw	Elaine	hel	Elezabethe	eli
Ebenezr	ebe	Edwarde	edw	Elam	ela	Elezabth	eli
Ebenzer	ebe	Edwardi	edw	Elaner	hel	Elezbeth	eli
Ebner	abn	Edwards	edw	Elanor	hel	Elezebeth	eli
Ecelia	cec	Edwardus	edw	Elayne	hel	Elfleda	alf
Eck	ale	Edwd	edw	Elaza	ele	Elfreda	alf
Ed	edw	Edwin	edw	Elazabeth	eli	Elfrida	alf
Eda	ada	Edwina	edw	Elba	elb	Elga	heg
Edan	edt	Edwn	edw	Elbertina	alb	Elgiva	elg
Edborough	edb	Edwood	edw	Elbright	alb	Elgra	heg
Edborowe	edb	Edword	edw	Elcaney	elk	Eli	elj
Edd	edw	Edwrd	edw	Elce	eli	Eliab	eli
Eddie	edw	Edwyne	edw	Elda	ald	Eliabeth	eli
Eddy	edw	Edyth	edt	Elden	eld	Elianor	hel
Ede	edt	Eeanor	hel	Eldine	eld	Elianora	hel
Eden	edt	Eelizabeth	eli	Elding	eld	Elias	elj
Edena	edt	Effie	eup	Eldon	eld	Elice	ali
Edeth	edt	Effim	eup	Eldred	ald	Elicia	ali
Edgar	edg	Effum	eup	Ele	hel	Elie	eli
Edie	edt	Effy	eup	Elean	hel	Elies	ali
Edina	edt	Egbert	egb	Eleanah	hel	Eliezer	ele
Edith	edt	Egerton	ege	Eleaner	hel	Eligah	elj
Editha	edt	Egidia	gia	Eleanor	hel	Eligha	elj
Edm	edw	Egidius	gia	Eleanora	hel	Elihu	elj
Edman	edw	Eglantine	egl	Eleasar	ele	Elija	elj
Edmand	edw	Eglentyne	egl	Eleazar	ele	Elijah	elj
Edmd	edw	Egnes	agn	Eleazer	ele	Elin	hel
Edmee	edw	Egness	agn	Eleener	hel	Elina	hel
Edmnd	edw	Ehster	est	Elein	hel	Elinar	hel
Edmond	edw	Eibhlin	hel	Elejea	elj	Elinda	lyn
Edmonde	edw	Eideard	edw	Elen	hel	Eliner	hel
Edmont	edw	Eileen	hel	Elena	hel	Elinn	hel
Edmund	edw	Eilidh	hel	Elener	hel	Elinnor	hel
Edmunde	edw	Eilish	eli	Eleni	hel	Elinor	hel
Edmundi	edw	Eilleen	hel	Elenner	hel	Elinore	hel
Edmundus	edw	Eilwen	eil	Elenor	hel	Elinour	hel
Edna	edn	Eilwyn	eil	Elenora	hel	Elioner	hel
Ednah	edn	Eily	hel	Elenr	hel	Elionor	hel

Eliot	elj	Elizea	ele	Elliott	elj	Elspt	eli
Elis	ali	Elizeabath	eli	Ellis	elj	Elspth	eli
Elisa	eli	Elizebath	eli	Ellisabeth	eli	Elton	elt
Elisab	eli	Elizebeth	eli	Ellison	ali	Eluned	elu
Elisabeh	eli	Elizebethae	eli	Elliss	ali	Elva	elv
Elisaberth	eli	Elizebth	eli	Elliza	eli	Elvera	aub
Elisabeth	eli	Elizer	ele	Ellizabeth	eli	Elvin	alw
Elisabetha	eli	Elizh	eli	Ellon	hel	Elvina	alw
Elisabethae	eli	Elizia	ele	Ellona	hel	Elvira	aub
Elisaeth	eli	Elizsabeth	eli	Elluned	elu	Elvis	elv
Elisah	eli	Elizt	eli	Ellunor	hel	Elwina	alw
Elisbeth	eli	Elizte	eli	Ellwyn	alw	Elwyn	alw
Elise	ali	Elizth	eli	Ellyn	hel	Ely	elj
Elisebeth	eli	Elkanah	elk	Ellynor	hel	Elyn	hel
Elish	eli	Ella	hel	Elma	wil	Elysabeth	eli
Elisha	elj	Ellalina	hel	Elmena	ame	Elysabethe	eli
Elison	ali	Ellan	hel	Elmer	elm	Elyzabeth	eli
Elisone	ali	Ellanor	hel	Elmina	ame	Elyzabetha	eli
Elispeth	eli	Ellas	ali	Elmo	era	Elyzabethe	eli
Elissa	eli	Ellceana	eli	Elmore	wil	Elz	eli
Elissabeth	eli	Elleanor	hel	Elmy	wil	Elza	eli
Elisth	eli	Ellece	ali	Elner	hel	Elzabath	eli
Elixabeth	eli	Ellen	hel	Elnor	hel	Elzabeth	eli
Eliz	eli	Ellena	hel	Elnye	hel	Elzbth	eli
Eliza	eli	Ellenar	hel	Eloisa	aly	Elzth	eli
Elizab	eli	Ellener	hel	Eloise	aly	Em	emm
Elizabath	eli	Ellenner	hel	Elon	hel	Ema	emm
Elizabeath	eli	Ellennor	hel	Elonar	hel	Emala	emm
Elizabeht	eli	Elleno	hel	Eloner	hel	Emaline	emm
Elizabella	eli	Ellenor	hel	Elonor	hel	Emaly	emm
Elizabet	eli	Ellery	ell	Elot	hel	Emanual	cma
Elizabeth	eli	Elles	ali	Elsa	eli	Emanuel	ema
Elizabetha	eli	Ellesebeth	eli	Elsabeth	eli	Emaretta	eme
Elizabethae	eli	Elless	ali	Elsabethe	eli	Emblem	emm
Elizabetham	eli	Elley	hel	Elsbeth	eli	Emblen	cmm
Elizabethe	eli	Elleypane	hel	Elsen	eli	Embler	emm
Elizabett	eli	Ellia	hel	Elseth	eli	Emblin	emm
Elizabh	eli	Elliane	hel	Elsie	eli	Embrose	amb
Elizabith	eli	Ellianor	hel	Elsiemeana	eli	Eme	emm
Elizabth	eli	Ellidth	hel	Elsp	eli	Emelena	emm
Elizaebth	eli	Ellie	hel	Elspa	eli	Emeley	emm
Elizaeth	eli	Ellimah	hel	Elspat	eli	Emeli	emm
Elizah	eli	Ellin	hel	Elspath	eli	Emelia	emm
Elizar	ele	Elline	hel	Elspet	eli	Emeline	emm
Elizath	eli	Elling	hel	Elspeth	eli	Emely	emm
Elizb	eli	Ellinn	hel	Elspie	eli	Emelyn	emm
Elizbeath	eli	Ellinor	hel	Elspit	eli	Emer	eme
Elizbeth	eli	Ellinr	hel	Elspith	eli	Emerald	esa
Elizbt	eli	Ellionora	hel	Elspitt	eli	Emeria	eme
Elizbth	eli	Elliot	elj	Elspot	eli		

25

First Names with Codes

Name	Code	Name	Code	Name	Code	Name	Code
Emerita	eme	Emn	emm	Erma	emm	Ethelwyn	eth
Emeritta	eme	Emne	emm	Ermintrude	erm	Etherton	ete
Emerson	eme	Emony	ism	Erna	ern	Ethne	ann
Emery	eme	Emota	emm	Ernest	ern	Ethra	eth
Emey	emm	Emott	emm	Ernestine	ern	Ethylinda	eth
Emiah	emm	Emotte	emm	Ernie	ern	Etta	hen
Emil	emm	Emrys	amb	Ernst	ern	Etty	hen
Emila	emm	Emuel	ema	Errol	har	Euan	ewe
Emile	emm	Emund	edw	Erskin	ers	Eubule	eub
Emilen	emm	Emy	emm	Erskine	ers	Euclid	euc
Emiley	emm	Emye	emm	Ervin	irv	Eudora	eud
Emilia	emm	Emylyn	emm	Erwin	irv	Euen	ewe
Emilie	emm	Ena	ann	Eryl	ery	Eufeme	eup
Emiliene	emm	Enas	anu	Eryn	eri	Eugene	eug
Emiline	emm	Enderby	end	Esabell	eli	Eugenia	eug
Emilly	emm	Eneas	anu	Esabella	eli	Eugenie	eug
Emily	emm	English	eng	Esabelle	eli	Eugine	eug
Emla	emm	Enice	eun	Esakiah	isa	Eulalia	eul
Emlen	emm	Enid	eni	Esan	esu	Eunice	eun
Emley	emm	Ennis	anu	Esau	esu	Euph	eup
Emlia	emm	Enoch	eno	Esaw	esu	Euphaim	eup
Emlin	emm	Enock	eno	Esebeloue	ese	Eupham	eup
Emly	emm	Enos	eno	Eshter	est	Euphame	eup
Emlyn	emm	Enrico	har	Esiau	esu	Euphan	eup
Emm	emm	Enry	har	Esibell	eli	Euphane	eup
Emma	emm	Enselin	lan	Esme	ism	Euphans	eup
Emmah	emm	Eoghan	eug	Esmee	ism	Euphean	eup
Emmala	emm	Eoghann	ewe	Esmeralda	esa	Euphem	eup
Emmalah	emm	Eoin	joh	Esmond	eso	Eupheme	eup
Emmaline	emm	Epaphroditus	aph	Ess	est	Euphemia	eup
Emmaly	emm	Eph	eph	Essex	ess	Euphemie	eup
Emmanuel	ema	Epham	eup	Essie	est	Euphen	eup
Emmanuelle	ema	Ephie	eup	Esta	est	Euphens	eup
Emmar	emm	Ephm	eph	Estelle	est	Euphimia	eup
Emmat	emm	Ephraim	eph	Ester	est	Euphin	eup
Emme	emm	Ephrain	eph	Estha	est	Euphmia	eup
Emmeat	emm	Ephram	eph	Esther	est	Euphrem	eup
Emmeby	emm	Ephrame	eph	Estrid	ast	Eusebius	eue
Emmelina	emm	Ephriam	eph	Etain	eti	Eustace	eus
Emmeline	emm	Ephy	eup	Etaoin	eti	Eustacia	eus
Emmely	emm	Eppie	eup	Ethan	eta	Eva	eve
Emmer	emm	Epsy	eup	Ethe	eth	Evadne	evd
Emmerson	eme	Erasmus	era	Ethel	eth	Evaline	eve
Emmet	emm	Eresken	ers	Ethelbert	eth	Evan	joh
Emmie	emm	Eric	fre	Ethelburg	eth	Evangeline	eve
Emmila	emm	Erica	fre	Etheldred	eth	Evans	joh
Emmily	emm	Erika	fre	Etheldreda	eth	Eve	eve
Emmot	emm	Erin	eri	Ethelia	eth	Eveleen	eve
Emmott	emm	Erismoth	era	Ethelinda	eth	Evelina	eve
Emmy	emm	Erle	ear	Ethelred	eth	Eveline	eve

Name	Code	Name	Code	Name	Code	Name	Code
Evelyn	eve	Farley	fal	Ffrancis	fra	Florrie	flo
Everalda	ave	Farmer	fam	Fhearghais	feg	Flory	flo
Everard	evr	Farnham	fan	Fiance	fra	Flossie	flo
Everet	evr	Farquhar	far	Fidel	fai	Flower	flo
Everhilda	ave	Farrell	frr	Fidelia	fai	Floy	flo
Everild	ave	Fawcett	faw	Fidelis	fai	Floyd	llo
Everitt	evr	Fawke	ful	Field	fie	Flurry	flo
Evie	eve	Fay	fai	Fielding	fie	Forbes	fob
Evita	eve	Faye	fai	Fife	fif	Forest	foe
Ewan	ewe	Fayth	fai	Filbert	phi	Forester	foe
Eward	edw	Faythe	fai	Fillida	phy	Forrest	foe
Ewart	evr	Feabe	phe	Fillis	phy	Forster	foe
Ewen	ewe	Feaby	phe	Filomana	pho	Fortunatus	for
Ewin	ewe	Fearchar	far	Filomena	pho	Fortune	for
Exannah	ann	Fearghus	feg	Findlay	fin	Foster	fos
Extop	chr	Feargus	feg	Findley	fin	Foulds	fou
Extopher	chr	Feather	fea	Finghin	flo	Foulk	ful
Eyde	edt	Featherstone	fea	Finlay	fin	Fountain	fon
Ez	ezr	Febee	phe	Finley	fin	Fowke	ful
Ezabella	eli	Febey	phe	Finola	fen	Fowler	fow
Ezakea	eze	Feby	phe	Fiona	fen	Fraces	fra
Ezakiah	eze	Federick	fre	Fionnghal	fen	Fraise	frs
Ezeikel	eze	Fedora	edw	Fionnlagh	fin	Fran	fra
Ezekiah	eze	Felice	phy	Firman	fir	Franc	fra
Ezekial	eze	Felicia	phy	Firmin	fir	Frances	fra
Ezekiel	eze	Felicity	phy	Firth	fih	Francesca	fra
Ezia	ish	Felix	phy	Fisher	fis	Francescus	fra
Eziekel	eze	Felles	phy	Fitch	fyt	Francess	fra
Ezit	eli	Fenella	fen	Fithian	viv	Francie	fra
Ezra	ezr	Fenna	fra	Fitz	fit	Francies	fra
Fabethy	phe	Fenne	fra	Fitzarthur	fit	Francine	fra
Fabia	fab	Fenton	fet	Fitzgerald	fit	Francis	fra
Fabian	fab	Fenwick	few	Fitzjohn	fit	Francisc	fra
Faby	phe	Feodora	edw	Fitzroy	fit	Francisca	fra
Faiethe	fai	Ferdenand	fer	Fitzwalter	fit	Franciscae	fra
Fairlay	fal	Ferdenando	fer	Flavia	fla	Francisci	fra
Faith	fai	Ferdinand	fer	Flaviana	fla	Francisco	fra
Faithful	fai	Ferdinanda	fer	Flavilla	fla	Franciscus	fra
Fancy	fra	Ferdinando	fer	Flavius	fla	Francises	fra
Fane	fra	Fereshteh	fee	Fletcher	fle	Franciska	fra
Faney	fra	Fergie	feg	Fleur	flo	Franciss	fra
Fann	fra	Fergus	feg	Flo	flo	Franck	fra
Fanna	fra	Ferguson	feg	Flora	flo	Francoise	fra
Fanney	fra	Fernleigh	fel	Floraidh	flo	Francs	fra
Fannie	fra	Fernley	fel	Florance	flo	Francus	fra
Fanny	fra	Feroniaca	ver	Florella	flo	Francys	fra
Fany	fra	Ferrand	fer	Florence	flo	Frang	fin
Faramond	faa	Ferry	fer	Florentina	flo	Frank	fra
Fardy	fer	Festus	fes	Florina	flo	Frankie	fra
Farewell	fae	Ffion	ros	Floris	flo	Franklin	fra

First Names with Codes

Franncis	fra	Fritz	fit	Garven	gav	Geoff	gef
Frans	fra	Fritzroy	fit	Garvis	gev	Geoffery	gef
Fransciscus	fra	Frizwith	fri	Gary	ger	Geoffray	gef
Franses	fra	Fryphena	try	Gascagne	gas	Geoffrey	gef
Fransis	fra	Frysewede	fri	Gascoigne	gas	Geoffry	gef
Franz	fra	Fryswyth	fri	Gascoygne	gas	Geofrey	gef
Fras	fra	Fulbert	phi	Gascoyne	gas	Geog	geo
Fraser	frs	Fulk	ful	Gaston	gas	Geogana	geo
Fraunc	fra	Fuller	fue	Gatesen	get	Geoganna	geo
Fraunce	fra	Fytch	fyt	Gateson	get	Geoge	geo
Fraunces	fra	Gabe	gab	Gatty	get	Geogre	geo
Frauncis	fra	Gabel	gab	Gavan	gav	Geor	geo
Fraunciscus	fra	Gabi	gab	Gaven	gav	Geordie	geo
Frazer	frs	Gabriel	gab	Gavin	gav	Georg	geo
Frcis	fra	Gabriell	gab	Gavyn	gav	Georgana	geo
Fred	fre	Gabriella	gab	Gawain	gav	Georganna	geo
Freda	fre	Gabrielle	gab	Gawen	gav	George	geo
Fredc	fre	Gabrilla	gab	Gawin	gav	Georgeana	geo
Freddy	fre	Gaby	gab	Gawn	gav	Georgeanna	geo
Frederic	fre	Gael	abi	Gay	gay	Georgeina	geo
Frederica	fre	Gaenor	gue	Gaye	gay	Georgena	geo
Frederich	fre	Gail	abi	Gayel	abi	Georges	geo
Frederick	fre	Gainerr	gue	Gayle	abi	Georgette	geo
Fredericus	fre	Gains	gue	Gaylord	gao	Georgia	geo
Fredica	fre	Gaius	gai	Gayna	gue	Georgiana	geo
Fredick	fre	Galahad	gal	Gaynah	gue	Georgianna	geo
Fredirick	fre	Gale	abi	Gayner	gue	Georgie	geo
Fredk	fre	Galfrid	gaf	Gaynor	gue	Georgiena	geo
Fredr	fre	Gam	gam	Ged	jed	Georgii	geo
Fredrck	fre	Gamaliel	gam	Geffraye	gef	Georgij	geo
Fredreck	fre	Gamaliell	gam	Geffrey	gef	Georgina	geo
Fredric	fre	Gamel	gam	Geiles	gie	Georgine	geo
Fredrica	fre	Gamma	gam	Geillis	gie	Georginia	geo
Fredrich	fre	Garald	ger	Geills	gie	Georginna	geo
Fredrick	fre	Gare	ger	Geils	gie	Georgium	geo
Fredrik	fre	Gareth	gar	Gelda	gia	Georgius	geo
Fredrk	fre	Garfield	gae	Gem	gam	Georguis	geo
Free	frm	Garland	gad	Gemelle	gam	Geraint	gei
Freeda	fre	Garmon	gma	Gemma	gam	Gerald	ger
Freedham	frm	Garner	gan	Gemmel	gam	Geraldine	ger
Freedom	frm	Garnet	wrr	Gena	eug	Geralt	ger
Freeman	frm	Garrat	ger	Gene	eug	Gerard	ger
Freida	fre	Garret	ger	Geneva	gue	Gerda	ged
Friday	fri	Garrett	ger	Genevieve	gue	Geri	ger
Frideswide	fri	Garrick	gac	Genevra	gue	Gerius	gev
Frideswyde	fri	Garrie	ger	Gent	gen	Germaine	gma
Frieda	fre	Garry	ger	Genty	gen	German	gma
Friend	frn	Garth	gar	Geo	geo	Geroge	geo
Friese	frs	Gartrite	get	Geoarge	geo	Gerome	jer
Friswith	fri	Gartrude	get	Geoe	geo	Gerrald	ger

Gerrard	ger	Gilius	gie	Gloria	glo	Grania	gin
Gerrold	ger	Gill	jul	Glorianna	glo	Grant	grn
Gerry	ger	Gillean	jul	Glorie	glo	Grantley	grt
Gersham	ges	Gilleasbaig	arc	Gloris	glo	Granville	grv
Gershom	ges	Gilleasbuig	arc	Glory	glo	Gratia	gra
Gershon	ges	Gilles	gie	Glyn	gly	Gratiae	gra
Gerson	ges	Gillet	jul	Glyndor	gly	Gray	gry
Gert	get	Gillian	jul	Glyndwr	gly	Green	gee
Gertie	get	Gillianne	jul	Glynis	gly	Greene	gee
Gertrude	get	Gillie	jul	Goddard	god	Greenwood	gee
Gerty	get	Gillies	gie	Godderd	god	Greer	gre
Geruase	gev	Gillot	jul	Godfery	gef	Greeta	mar
Geruis	gev	Gillson	jul	Godfray	gef	Greg	gre
Gervas	gev	Gillyanne	jul	Godfrey	gef	Gregery	gre
Gervase	gev	Gilo	gie	Godfrus	gef	Gregg	gre
Gervis	gev	Gilroy	gir	Godfry	gef	Gregor	gre
Gervise	gev	Gilse	gie	Godith	gow	Gregorij	gre
Geth	gte	Gilson	jul	Godiva	gef	Gregory	gre
Gethen	gte	Gina	reg	Godly	gow	Grenne	gee
Gethin	gte	Ginette	gue	Godlyne	gow	Grenville	grv
Gethro	geh	Ginevra	gue	Godric	gow	Gresham	gea
Geve	gef	Ginger	vir	Godwin	gow	Greta	mar
Ghislaine	gis	Ginnette	gue	Goerge	geo	Gretchen	mar
Gias	gai	Ginnie	vir	Goergeanna	geo	Gretel	mar
Gib	gil	Ginny	eug	Golden	goe	Gretta	mar
Gibbie	gil	Gipsy	gip	Goldie	goe	Greville	grl
Gibbon	gil	Girsal	grs	Golding	goe	Grey	gry
Gibbun	gil	Girsall	grs	Goldwin	goe	Griesel	grs
Gibby	gil	Girsel	grs	Goliath	gol	Griff	gri
Gibe	gil	Girtrude	get	Golliath	gol	Griffes	gri
Gibeon	gil	Girzel	grs	Gomer	gom	Griffin	gri
Gibson	gil	Girzil	grs	Goodeth	gow	Griffith	gri
Gibun	gil	Gisela	gis	Goodman	goa	Grigor	gre
Gideon	gid	Gisele	gis	Gordan	gor	Grimbald	grm
Giff	gef	Gita	brd	Gorden	gor	Grimshaw	grw
Gifford	gif	Githa	git	Gordie	gor	Grisal	grs
Gilbert	gil	Gladis	cld	Gordon	gor	Grisel	grs
Gilberta	gil	Gladness	cld	Gorg	geo	Griselda	grs
Gilbertus	gil	Gladstone	gla	Gorge	geo	Grisell	grs
Gilbride	gil	Gladuse	cld	Goronwy	gon	Grisiel	grs
Gilda	gia	Gladwys	cld	Grace	gra	Grisiell	grs
Gilder	gia	Gladys	cld	Gracey	gra	Grisigion	chy
Gildero	gir	Glanville	gln	Gracia	gra	Grissal	grs
Gilderoy	gir	Glen	gwe	Gracie	gra	Grissall	grs
Gildray	gir	Glenda	gwe	Gracilia	gra	Grissel	grs
Gildri	gir	Glenn	gwe	Graeme	grh	Grissell	grs
Gildroy	gir	Glenna	gwe	Graham	grh	Grissil	grs
Gileas	gie	Glennis	gly	Grahame	grh	Grissill	grs
Giles	gie	Glenys	gly	Grainne	gin	Grizal	grs
Gilian	jul	Glinys	gly	Grainnia	gin	Grizall	grs

First Names with Codes

Name	Code	Name	Code	Name	Code	Name	Code
Grizel	grs	Gwendoline	gwe	Hamet	ham	Hardisty	hrd
Grizell	grs	Gwendolyn	gwe	Hamilton	hao	Hardy	hrd
Grizzel	grs	Gwendy	gwe	Hamish	jam	Hardyman	hrd
Grizzle	grs	Gweneth	gwe	Hamlet	ham	Hargrave	has
Grover	gro	Gwenfrewi	win	Hamlin	ham	Hargreaves	has
Groves	gro	Gwenhwyfar	gue	Hamlyn	ham	Haribert	alb
Gruffold	gri	Gwenillian	gwe	Hammet	ham	Hariet	hen
Gruffydd	gri	Gwenllean	gwe	Hammond	ham	Hariett	hen
Guendolen	gwe	Gwenllian	gwe	Hamnet	ham	Hariot	hen
Guenevere	gue	Gwenn	gwe	Hamo	ham	Hariott	hen
Guenor	gue	Gwenneth	gwe	Hamon	ham	Harley	hrl
Guglielma	wil	Gwennie	gwe	Hamond	ham	Harman	hem
Guido	guy	Gwenyth	gwe	Hamphris	phy	Harold	har
Guildford	gul	Gwilliam	wil	Hampless	phy	Haroldene	har
Guilford	gul	Gwilym	wil	Hampliss	phy	Harper	hra
Guilielmus	wil	Gwinefried	win	Han	ann	Harrat	hen
Guilihelmi	wil	Gwladys	cld	Hana	ann	Harray	har
Guinevere	gue	Gwyn	gwe	Hanah	ann	Harreit	hen
Guiscard	gui	Gwyneth	gwe	Hanaha	ann	Harreitt	hen
Gul	wil	Gwynne	gwe	Hanam	ann	Harret	hen
Gulelmus	wil	Gylbert	gil	Hand	hae	Harrett	hen
Guliel	wil	Gyles	gie	Handel	had	Harrey	har
Gulielimus	wil	Gyllon	gie	Handley	hae	Harriat	hen
Guliell	wil	Hab	rob	Hane	ann	Harriatt	hen
Guliellmi	wil	Habby	rob	Hanh	ann	Harrie	har
Guliellmus	wil	Haburd	alb	Hank	har	Harriet	hen
Gulielm	wil	Hadassah	est	Hanley	hae	Harriete	hen
Gulielmi	wil	Haddon	aid	Hann	ann	Harriett	hen
Gulielmu	wil	Hadrian	adr	Hanna	ann	Harrietta	hen
Gulielmum	wil	Hadyn	aid	Hannabell	aml	Harriette	hen
Gulielmus	wil	Hagar	hag	Hannagh	ann	Harrington	hrr
Gulih	wil	Haggar	hag	Hannah	ann	Harriot	hen
Gulmi	wil	Haidee	hai	Hannar	hel	Harriott	hen
Gunilda	gun	Hailey	har	Hanne	ann	Harris	har
Gunnell	gun	Haines	hia	Hanner	hel	Harrison	har
Gurney	gur	Hal	har	Hannh	ann	Harrit	hen
Gus	aug	Halbert	alb	Hannibal	han	Harritt	hen
Gussie	aug	Halcyon	hac	Hannibel	han	Harrold	har
Gustas	aug	Haldane	hal	Hannie	ann	Harrop	hro
Gustav	aug	Haley	har	Hanorah	hel	Harrot	hen
Gustave	aug	Halford	haf	Hanry	har	Harrott	hen
Gustavus	aug	Halfred	alf	Hans	joh	Harrt	hen
Guy	guy	Halina	hel	Hanson	joh	Harruet	hen
Guyat	guy	Hall	har	Happy	hap	Harry	har
Guyryve	guy	Hallam	haa	Haralda	har	Harrye	har
Gwallter	wal	Hallen	hel	Haray	har	Hart	hen
Gwalter	wal	Hallewell	hei	Harbert	alb	Hartley	hat
Gwen	gwe	Halley	har	Harbord	alb	Harty	hen
Gwenda	gwe	Ham	ham	Harcourt	hau	Harvet	hav
Gwendolen	gwe	Hamby	ham	Harden	hrd	Harvey	hav

Harwood	haw	Helenor	hel	Henrey	har	Hessie	est
Hary	har	Helewise	aly	Henri	har	Hessy	est
Haryat	hen	Helga	heg	Henriatta	hen	Hester	est
Haselwood	haz	Helin	hel	Henrici	har	Hesther	est
Hastings	hsa	Helina	hel	Henricus	har	Hetta	hew
Hattie	hen	Heline	hel	Henrie	har	Hette	hen
Hatty	hen	Helison	hel	Henrieta	hen	Hettie	hen
Haugh	hua	Hell	hel	Henrietta	hen	Hetty	hen
Havelock	hak	Hellan	hel	Henriette	hen	Heugh	hug
Hawthorn	hah	Hellein	hel	Henrik	har	Hevah	eve
Hawthorne	hah	Hellen	hel	Henritta	hen	Hew	hug
Haxby	hax	Hellena	hel	Henry	har	Hewet	hug
Haydn	aid	Hellenae	hel	Henrye	har	Hewgh	hug
Haydon	aid	Hellence	hel	Henryk	har	Hewghe	hug
Hayley	hay	Hellewell	hei	Henury	har	Hewin	hug
Hayward	hya	Hellin	hel	Heny	har	Hewitt	hug
Hayyim	hym	Helliwell	hei	Hephizibah	hep	Hez	hez
Hazael	haz	Hellon	hel	Hephsibah	hep	Hezekiah	hez
Hazal	haz	Helma	wil	Hephzabah	hep	Hezia	ish
Hazel	haz	Helyn	hel	Hephzebah	hep	Heziah	ish
Hazeline	haz	Hen	har	Hephzebay	hep	Hibernia	eri
Hazell	haz	Henaghan	hne	Hephzibah	hep	Hick	ric
Hazelle	haz	Henary	har	Hepsey	hep	Hicket	ric
Headley	hed	Henderson	har	Hepsibah	hep	Hiedi	ada
Heath	hea	Hendre	har	Hepsie	hep	Hilary	hil
Heather	hea	Hendrie	har	Hepsy	hep	Hilda	hid
Heaton	het	Hendrik	har	Hepzabah	hep	Hilde	hid
Hebden	hbe	Hendry	har	Hepzibah	hep	Hildebrand	hid
Hebdon	hbe	Heneage	hne	Hepzibeth	hep	Hildegard	hid
Hebe	heb	Heneretta	hen	Herald	har	Hildred	hid
Heber	heb	Henerey	har	Herbert	alb	Hill	hil
Hebor	heb	Henerici	har	Herbertus	alb	Hillary	hil
Hector	hec	Henericus	har	Herbet	alb	Hillery	hil
Hectorina	hec	Henerietta	hen	Herbit	alb	Hilma	wil
Hedda	hew	Henerita	hen	Hercula	her	Hilorie	hil
Hedley	hed	Heneritta	hen	Hercules	her	Hilton	hit
Hedly	hed	Henery	har	Hereward	hee	Hindrie	har
Hedwig	hew	Henerye	har	Heriot	hen	Hippolyta	hip
Hedy	hew	Henie	har	Herman	hem	Hippolyte	hip
Heenery	har	Heniretta	hen	Hermia	hem	Hiram	hir
Heidi	ada	Henley	hey	Hermoine	hem	Hirom	hir
Helah	hel	Hennerie	har	Hermon	hem	Hitch	ric
Helean	hel	Hennery	har	Hero	hre	Hlen	hel
Helein	hel	Henney	har	Herod	heo	Hnry	har
Helen	hel	Hennry	har	Herriet	hen	Hny	har
Helena	hel	Henny	hen	Herriett	hen	Hob	rob
Helenam	hel	Henor	har	Herriot	hen	Hobart	alb
Helene	hel	Henr	har	Hervey	hav	Hobson	rob
Helener	hel	Henreitta	hen	Heryc	har	Hod	hor
Helenn	hel	Henretta	hen	Hesketh	hes	Hodge	rog

Name	Code	Name	Code	Name	Code	Name	Code
Hodgkin	rog	Howard	hoa	Hyrum	hir	Ingeborg	ina
Hodgson	rog	Howel	how	Hywel	how	Ingham	inh
Hodson	rog	Howell	how	Iago	jam	Ingmar	ing
Hoel	how	Hry	har	Iain	joh	Ingraham	ing
Holden	hod	Hubbard	alb	Ian	joh	Ingram	ing
Holland	hol	Hubert	alb	Ianthe	ian	Ingrid	ing
Holley	hol	Hudde	ric	Iassabel	eli	Inigo	ign
Hollie	hol	Hudson	ric	Ib	eli	Innes	ine
Hollis	hol	Huey	hug	Ibbie	eli	Innis	ine
Holly	hol	Hugh	hug	Icarus	ica	Innocent	inn
Holman	hom	Hughe	hug	Ichabod	ich	Ino	chr
Holmes	hom	Hughes	hug	Ida	ida	Iohn	joh
Homer	hom	Hughey	hug	Idabell	ida	Iola	edw
Homfrey	hum	Hughie	hug	Idonia	ido	Iolo	edw
Hon	hon	Hughina	hug	Idris	idr	Iomhair	ivr
Honer	hel	Hugo	hug	Idwal	idw	Iomhar	ivr
Honey	hon	Hugoi	hug	Ieashia	aih	Iona	ion
Honner	hel	Hugois	hug	Iesha	aih	Iorwerth	edw
Honnor	hel	Hugonis	hug	Iestin	jus	Ira	ira
Honnour	hel	Huisdean	hug	Iestyn	jus	Irena	ire
Honor	hel	Hulda	hul	Ieuan	joh	Irene	ire
Honora	hel	Huldah	hul	Ifor	ivr	Iris	iri
Honorah	hel	Humfrey	hum	Ignacious	ign	Irma	emm
Honore	hel	Humfridus	hum	Ignas	ign	Irona	ion
Honoria	hel	Humfry	hum	Ignatia	ign	Irvin	irv
Honour	hel	Humph	hum	Ignatious	ign	Irvine	irv
Hope	hop	Humphery	hum	Ignatius	ign	Irving	irv
Hopeful	hop	Humphrey	hum	Igor	ina	Irwin	irv
Hopestill	hop	Humphry	hum	Ike	isa	Isa	eli
Hopkin	rob	Humphrye	hum	Ikey	isa	Isaac	isa
Horace	hor	Hunter	hun	Ilean	hel	Isaacc	isa
Horanah	aru	Huntly	hun	Ileen	hel	Isaack	isa
Horatia	hor	Huram	hir	Ilene	hel	Isaacs	isa
Horatio	hor	Hurbert	alb	Illingworth	ili	Isaah	ish
Horatius	hor	Hurrish	hor	Illtyd	ill	Isaak	isa
Hornby	hob	Hutchinson	hug	Ilma	wil	Isab	eli
Horne	hoe	Huw	hug	Ilse	eli	Isaballa	eli
Horner	hoe	Hwmffrey	hum	Ima	emm	Isabel	eli
Hornsby	hob	Hwmfrey	hum	Imalda	ima	Isabela	eli
Horrace	hor	Hy	hir	Imally	emm	Isabell	eli
Horry	hor	Hyacinth	cyn	Imblen	emm	Isabella	eli
Horsell	hof	Hyacinthe	cyn	Imelda	ima	Isabellah	eli
Horsfall	hof	Hyam	hir	Immanuel	ema	Isabelle	eli
Hortensia	hot	Hyla	hel	Imogen	imo	Isabla	eli
Hosanna	hos	Hylda	hid	Imogene	imo	Isable	eli
Hosannah	hos	Hylton	hit	Imogine	imo	Isabol	eli
Hosen	hos	Hyman	hym	Ina	chr	Isac	isa
Hoseph	jos	Hymen	hym	Inga	ina	Isacc	isa
Hoson	hos	Hymie	hym	Ingaret	anc	Isach	isa
How	hug	Hypatia	hyp	Inge	ina	Isack	isa

Name	Code	Name	Code	Name	Code	Name	Code
Isacke	isa	Issoble	eli	Jacob	jca	Janes	jam
Isador	isi	Issy	isr	Jacoba	jca	Janessa	joa
Isadora	isi	Ithel	ith	Jacobi	jca	Janet	joa
Isah	ish	Iva	iva	Jacobina	jca	Janeta	joa
Isaiah	ish	Ivah	iva	Jacobine	jca	Janett	joa
Isaic	isa	Ivan	joh	Jacobj	jca	Janetta	joa
Isaih	ish	Ivana	joh	Jacobus	jca	Janette	joa
Isake	isa	Iver	ivr	Jacolyn	jac	Janey	joa
Isarel	isr	Iverna	eri	Jacqualynn	jac	Janice	joa
Isbald	eli	Ives	ivo	Jacqueline	jac	Janie	joa
Isbel	eli	Iveson	ivr	Jacquelyn	jac	Janis	joa
Isbell	eli	Ivette	ivo	Jacques	jam	Janit	joa
Isbella	eli	Ivie	ivr	Jacquetta	jac	Jann	joa
Iseabail	eli	Ivo	ivo	Jacqui	jac	Jannat	joa
Iseac	isa	Ivon	ivo	Jade	jad	Janne	joa
Isebella	eli	Ivor	ivr	Jael	jae	Janner	joh
Iseral	isr	Ivoreen	ivr	Jaell	jae	Jannet	joa
Ishbel	eli	Ivorine	ivr	Jaen	joa	Jannett	joa
Ishmael	ism	Ivy	ivr	Jaes	jam	Jannetta	joa
Isiah	ish	Izaak	isa	Jago	jam	Jannette	joa
Isibel	eli	Izaat	isa	Jaime	jam	Jannot	joa
Isible	eli	Izabel	eli	Jain	joa	Jannott	joa
Isidore	isi	Izabell	eli	Jaine	joa	Janot	joa
Isla	eli	Izabella	eli	Jaines	joa	Jant	joa
Ismay	ism	Izable	eli	Jake	jca	Japheth	jep
Ismena	ism	Izaell	eli	Jam	jam	Jaquelina	jac
Ismenia	ism	Izot	iso	Jamar	jam	Jaqueline	jac
Isobel	eli	Izzy	isr	Jame	jam	Jared	jar
Isobell	eli	Ja	jam	James	jam	Jarius	jer
Isobella	eli	Jabas	jab	Jamesin	jam	Jarman	gma
Isoble	eli	Jabaz	jab	Jamesina	jam	Jaro	jar
Isolda	iso	Jabe	jab	Jamesing	jam	Jarvis	gev
Isolde	iso	Jaber	jab	Jameson	jam	Jas	jam
Isolte	iso	Jabes	jab	Jamesyng	jam	Jasmin	jan
Isot	iso	Jabesh	jab	Jamie	jam	Jasmine	jan
Isott	iso	Jabey	jab	Jamieson	jam	Jason	jas
Israel	isr	Jabez	jab	Jamima	jam	Jasper	jap
Israell	isr	Jabus	jab	Jamis	jam	Jasse	jes
Isreal	isr	Jacabus	jca	Jammey	jam	Javan	jav
Issa	eli	Jacaline	jac	Jammima	jam	Javin	jav
Issabel	eli	Jacalyn	jac	Jams	jam	Javon	jav
Issabell	eli	Jacinta	cyn	Jamsie	jam	Jay	jam
Issabella	eli	Jacinth	cyn	Jan	joh	Jayme	jam
Issabelle	eli	Jacintha	cyn	Jana	joa	Jayne	joa
Issac	isa	Jack	joh	Janae	joa	Jayson	jas
Issacar	isa	Jackie	jac	Janam	joa	Jeames	jam
Issachar	isa	Jackobenna	jca	Janat	joa	Jean	joa
Issobel	eli	Jackson	jak	Jane	joa	Jeane	joa
Issobell	eli	Jacky	jac	Janell	joa	Jeanette	joa
Issobella	eli	Jaclyn	jac	Janene	joa	Jeanie	joa

First Names with Codes

Name	Code	Name	Code	Name	Code	Name	Code
Jeanit	joa	Jenney	joa	Jestine	jus	Joanna	joa
Jeanne	joa	Jennie	gue	Jethro	jet	Joannae	joa
Jeannie	joa	Jennifer	gue	Jeturah	jet	Joannah	joa
Jeannit	joa	Jennit	joa	Jeuis	jew	Joanne	joa
Jebez	jab	Jennitt	joa	Jevon	joh	Joannes	joa
Jed	jed	Jenny	gue	Jewel	joe	Joannis	joa
Jeddia	jed	Jeoffrey	gef	Jewell	joe	Joas	joa
Jedidiah	jed	Jeoyse	joy	Jewes	jew	Job	job
Jefery	gef	Jephtha	jep	Jewess	jew	Jobe	job
Jeff	gef	Jephthah	jep	Jewett	jul	Jobey	job
Jefferey	gef	Jephunneth	jep	Jezabell	jez	Jobie	job
Jefferies	gef	Jeptha	jep	Jezebel	jez	Joby	job
Jefferson	gef	Jerald	ger	Jezebell	jez	Jocasta	jco
Jeffery	gef	Jeraldine	ger	Jhn	joh	Jocelin	joy
Jeffray	gef	Jeramye	jer	Jho	joh	Jocelyn	joy
Jeffree	gef	Jereh	jer	Jhoanna	joa	Jochem	joc
Jeffrey	gef	Jeremh	jer	Jhohan	joa	Jock	joh
Jeffrie	gef	Jeremia	jer	Jhon	joh	Joclyn	joy
Jeffry	gef	Jeremiah	jer	Jhone	joh	Jodie	jui
Jehu	jeh	Jeremie	jer	Jhonn	joh	Joe	jos
Jehudijah	jeh	Jeremy	jer	Jiles	gie	Joel	joe
Jellian	jul	Jerimiah	jer	Jill	jul	Joene	joa
Jem	jam	Jerman	gma	Jillain	jul	Joey	jos
Jemima	jam	Jermiah	jer	Jillet	jul	Joffre	jof
Jemimah	jam	Jermyn	gma	Jillian	jul	Joh	joh
Jemina	jam	Jerold	ger	Jillianne	jul	Johaes	joa
Jemma	jam	Jerome	jer	Jim	jam	Johais	joa
Jemmima	jam	Jerrold	ger	Jimima	jam	Johames	joa
Jemmina	jam	Jerry	jer	Jimmima	jam	Johan	joa
Jemmy	jam	Jervas	gev	Jimminer	jam	Johana	joa
Jen	joh	Jervase	gev	Jimmy	jam	Johanah	joa
Jenat	joa	Jervice	gev	Jinney	joa	Johane	joa
Jenefer	gue	Jervis	gev	Jinny	joa	Johanem	joa
Jenet	joa	Jese	jes	Jirmirna	jam	Johanes	joa
Jeneta	joa	Jesea	jes	Jm	jam	Johaneta	joa
Jenete	joa	Jeseph	jos	Jn	joh	Johani	joa
Jenett	joa	Jesiah	jou	Jnet	joa	Johanis	joa
Jenette	joa	Jesie	jes	Jno	joh	Johanj	joa
Jeney	joa	Jesmond	ism	Jo	jos	Johann	joa
Jenico	ign	Jesper	jap	Joab	job	Johanna	joa
Jenifer	gue	Jess	jes	Joachim	joc	Johannah	joa
Jenit	joa	Jessa	jes	Joah	jho	Johannas	joa
Jenitt	joa	Jessamine	jan	Joan	joa	Johanne	joa
Jenkin	joh	Jesse	jes	Joana	joa	Johannem	joa
Jenkins	joh	Jessee	jes	Joanah	joa	Johannes	joa
Jenna	joa	Jesses	jes	Joane	joa	Johanney	joa
Jennat	joa	Jessey	jes	Joanes	joa	Johannie	joa
Jennet	joa	Jessica	jes	Joanet	joa	Johannis	joa
Jennett	joa	Jessie	jes	Joanis	joa	Johanus	joa
Jennetta	joa	Jessy	jes	Joann	joa	Johas	joa

Johe	jos	Jonothon	joh	Jowett	jul	Justine	jus
Johes	jos	Jonquil	joq	Joy	joy	Justinian	jus
Johh	jos	Jony	joh	Joyce	joy	Juverna	eri
Johis	jos	Jonye	joh	Joycelyn	joy	Kalvin	kel
John	joh	Joph	jos	Joziah	jou	Kane	kan
Johna	joh	Jopseph	jos	Jseph	jos	Kara	car
Johnanna	joa	Jordan	jor	Ju	jui	Karen	kee
Johnathan	joh	Jos	jos	Juanita	joa	Karena	kee
Johnathon	joh	Josa	jos	Jubal	jub	Karina	kee
Johne	joh	Josalene	joy	Jubilee	jub	Karl	cha
Johnes	joh	Joscelin	joy	Juda	jud	Karleen	cao
Johnis	joh	Jose	jos	Judah	jud	Karol	cao
Johnne	joh	Joseah	jou	Judas	jud	Karrenappuch	kee
Johnny	joh	Joseh	jos	Judath	jul	Karrenhappuch	kee
Johns	joh	Joselene	joy	Judd	jor	Kasia	kez
Johnson	joh	Josep	jos	Jude	jud	Kass	kat
Johnsten	joh	Joseph	jos	Judeth	jui	Katarina	kat
Johnston	joh	Josepha	jos	Judia	jud	Kate	kat
Johnstone	joh	Josephe	jos	Judith	jui	Kath	kat
Johnthan	joh	Josephene	jos	Judithe	jui	Kathar	kat
Johs	jos	Josephi	jos	Judy	jui	Katharen	kat
Joice	joy	Josephine	jos	Juet	jul	Katharin	kat
Joie	joy	Josephn	jos	Juetta	jul	Katharine	kat
Jolyon	jul	Josephus	jos	Juilea	jul	Katharyne	kat
Jon	joh	Joses	jos	Jule	jul	Kathe	kat
Jona	joh	Josh	jou	Jules	jul	Katheraine	kat
Jonah	joh	Joshah	jou	Juley	jul	Katheran	kat
Jonas	joh	Josheph	jos	Julia	jul	Katherein	kat
Jonat	joa	Joshua	jou	Juliah	jul	Katheren	kat
Jonath	joh	Joshuah	jou	Julian	jul	Katherene	kat
Jonatha	joh	Joshue	jou	Juliana	jul	Katherin	kat
Jonathan	joh	Josia	jou	Juliann	jul	Katherina	kat
Jonathania	joh	Josiah	jou	Julianna	jul	Katherinam	kat
Jonathanis	joh	Josias	jou	Julias	jul	Katherine	kat
Jonathas	joh	Josie	jos	Julie	jul	Kathern	kat
Jonathen	joh	Josilene	joy	Julielmus	jul	Katherne	kat
Jonathn	joh	Josp	jos	Julien	jul	Katheryn	kat
Jonathon	joh	Jospeh	jos	Juliet	jul	Katheryne	kat
Jone	joa	Josph	jos	Julius	jul	Kathleen	kat
Joneh	joh	Joss	joy	Jullian	jul	Kathlyn	kat
Jones	joa	Josse	joy	July	jul	Kathorne	kat
Jonet	joa	Jossiah	jou	Julyan	jul	Kathr	kat
Jonett	joa	Josslyn	joy	Julyen	jul	Kathren	kat
Jonie	joh	Jossua	jou	June	jun	Kathrene	kat
Jonn	joh	Josua	jou	Juno	win	Kathrin	kat
Jonnet	joa	Josuah	jou	Jusica	jes	Kathrinae	kat
Jonnett	joa	Josuha	jou	Justice	jut	Kathrine	kat
Jonney	joh	Jotham	jot	Justillian	jus	Kathron	kat
Jonny	joh	Jothin	jot	Justin	jus	Kathryn	kat
Jonothan	joh	Jouls	jul	Justina	jus	Katie	kat

First Names with Codes

Name	Code	Name	Code	Name	Code	Name	Code
Katina	kat	Kennedy	ked	Kirby	kib	Lancelin	lan
Katran	kat	Kenneth	ken	Kirk	kir	Lanceliott	lan
Katren	kat	Kennice	ken	Kirstan	chr	Lancelot	lan
Katrena	kat	Kenny	ken	Kirstane	chr	Lancelott	lan
Katrina	kat	Kenrick	ker	Kirsten	chr	Lancelt	lan
Katrine	kat	Kent	ket	Kirsty	chr	Lanceolett	lan
Kay	kat	Kentigern	ket	Kirton	kit	Lane	hel
Kaylee	kyl	Kenton	keo	Kissie	kez	Langford	lag
Kayley	kyl	Kenza	ken	Kit	chr	Lannclot	lan
Kazia	kez	Kerah	kee	Kittey	kat	Lanty	lau
Keala	kyl	Keren	kee	Kitty	kat	Lara	lar
Kealey	kyl	Kerenhappuch	kee	Kiturah	keu	Larace	lau
Kealy	kyl	Keri	kee	Kity	kat	Larance	lau
Keathran	kat	Keria	kee	Kizia	kez	Larence	lau
Keathren	kat	Kermit	deo	Kizzie	kez	Lari	lau
Keble	keb	Kerr	kee	Knight	kni	Larisa	lar
Keeley	kyl	Kerri	kee	Kora	cor	Larrence	lau
Keelie	kyl	Kerrick	ker	Korrein	cor	Larry	lau
Keeling	kyl	Kerrie	kee	Kris	chr	Latitia	let
Keely	kyl	Kerry	kee	Kristina	chr	Lauchlan	lac
Keighley	kyl	Kerstie	chr	Kristoffer	chr	Lauchlen	lac
Keiley	kyl	Kersty	chr	Kurt	cou	Lauchlin	lac
Keilly	kyl	Kerziah	kez	Kyle	kyl	Laughlan	lac
Keily	kyl	Kesia	kez	Kylee	kyl	Laughlin	lac
Keir	kie	Kesiah	kez	Kylie	kyl	Laughline	lac
Keira	kie	Kessiah	kez	Kym	kim	Launce	lan
Keiran	kie	Kester	chr	Kyran	kie	Launceliot	lan
Keith	kei	Kethiah	kez	Laban	lab	Launcelot	lan
Kelcey	kes	Kethrain	kat	Labina	lav	Laura	lau
Kellem	ken	Kethrin	kat	Laccheus	zac	Lauranc	lau
Kelley	kyl	Kettura	keu	Lacey	lca	Laurance	lau
Kellie	kyl	Ketty	kat	Lachlain	lac	Laureance	lau
Kelly	kyl	Keturah	keu	Lachlan	lac	Laureen	lau
Kelsa	kes	Kevan	ken	Lachland	lac	Laurel	lau
Kelsey	kes	Keverne	ken	Lachlanina	lac	Lauren	lau
Kelsie	kes	Kevin	ken	Lachlon	lac	Laurena	lau
Kelvin	kel	Kezia	kez	Lachunn	lac	Laurence	lau
Kelvyn	kel	Keziah	kez	Lacy	lca	Laurentius	lau
Kem	ken	Kidd	chr	Ladia	lad	Laurentus	lau
Ken	ken	Kieley	kyl	Lady	lad	Lauretta	lau
Kena	ken	Kieli	kyl	Laetitia	let	Laurice	lau
Kendal	kea	Kiera	kie	Laila	lel	Laurie	lau
Kendall	kea	Kieran	kie	Lallie	eul	Lauriman	lau
Kendra	ken	Kiley	kyl	Lambard	lam	Laurina	lau
Kendrick	ker	Kim	kim	Lambert	lam	Laurinda	lau
Kenelm	ken	Kimberley	kim	Lambin	lam	Laurine	lau
Keneme	ken	Kimberly	kim	Lament	lao	Lavena	lav
Kenerick	ker	King	kin	Lamont	lao	Lavenia	lav
Kenhelm	ken	Kingsley	kin	Lana	hel	Laverne	lae
Kenia	ken	Kingston	kin	Lance	lan	Lavia	lav

36

Name	Code	Name	Code	Name	Code	Name	Code
Lavina	lav	Lennard	leo	Lewellen	lle	Lindon	lyo
Laviner	lav	Lennox	len	Lewellin	lle	Lindsay	lid
Lavinia	lav	Lenny	leo	Lewes	lew	Lindsey	lid
Lavinie	lav	Lenoard	leo	Lewin	lwe	Lindy	lyn
Law	lau	Lenora	hel	Lewis	lew	Lindzy	lid
Lawe	lau	Lenord	leo	Lewisa	lew	Linnet	lyn
Lawranc	lau	Lenore	hel	Lewys	lew	Linney	lyn
Lawrance	lau	Leo	leo	Lex	ale	Linsay	lid
Lawrenc	lau	Leon	leo	Lexi	ale	Linsey	lid
Lawrence	lau	Leona	leo	Leyla	lel	Linton	lit
Lawrencii	lau	Leonara	hel	Leyton	lay	Linus	lin
Lawrentii	lau	Leonard	leo	Liam	wil	Linzi	lid
Lawrentius	lau	Leonardus	leo	Lianne	jul	Lionel	leo
Lawria	lau	Leonie	leo	Libbie	eli	Lisa	eli
Lawrie	lau	Leonora	hel	Libby	eli	Lisbeth	eli
Lawson	lau	Leopold	leo	Libella	eli	Lise	eli
Lawton	law	Leroy	ler	Lida	lyd	Lisette	eli
Layfield	laf	Les	les	Lidda	lyd	Lisle	lya
Layland	lal	Lesley	les	Lidday	lyd	Lissie	eli
Layton	lay	Leslie	les	Liddayay	lyd	Lister	lis
Lazarus	ele	Lesly	les	Liddia	lyd	Lititia	let
Lea	leh	Lester	lee	Liddiah	lyd	Livie	oli
Leah	leh	Leta	let	Liddy	lyd	Livina	lav
Leanda	lea	Letesse	let	Lide	lyd	Livinia	lav
Leander	lea	Letice	let	Lidia	lyd	Liza	eli
Leandra	lea	Leticia	let	Lidya	lyd	Lizbeth	eli
Leanne	jul	Letita	let	Lieser	eli	Lizey	eli
Leanora	hel	Letitia	let	Lil	lel	Lizy	eli
Lear	lly	Letittia	let	Lila	lel	Lizzee	eli
Leatitia	let	Lettesia	let	Lilas	lel	Lizzie	eli
Leda	alf	Lettia	let	Lilia	lel	Lizzy	eli
Ledah	lyd	Lettice	let	Liliah	lel	Llewelin	lle
Ledea	lyd	Letticia	let	Lilian	lel	Llewellin	lle
Lee	leh	Lettisia	let	Lilias	lel	Llewellyn	lle
Lees	leh	Lettitia	let	Lilith	lil	Llewelyn	lle
Leigh	leh	Lettuce	let	Lilius	lel	Lloyd	llo
Leighton	lay	Letty	let	Lilla	lel	Llyr	lly
Leila	lel	Leucy	luc	Lillah	lel	Llywelyn	lle
Lelah	lel	Leuisa	lew	Lillas	lel	Loanna	joa
Lelia	lel	Leusia	lew	Lilley	lel	Lob	lob
Lellie	lel	Levena	lav	Lillian	lel	Lochlan	lac
Lem	lem	Levener	lav	Lillias	lel	Lodowick	lod
Lemmy	lem	Levenia	lav	Lilliaz	lel	Loftas	lof
Lemuel	lem	Levi	lev	Lillie	lel	Lofthouse	lof
Len	leo	Levia	lev	Lilly	lel	Loftus	lof
Lena	hel	Levina	lav	Lily	lel	Lois	lew
Lenard	leo	Levinia	lav	Lina	cao	Lola	dol
Lenda	leo	Levins	lev	Lincoln	lic	Lolita	dol
Leneazer	ele	Levy	lev	Linda	lyn	Lolly	lau
Lenna	leo	Lew	lew	Linden	lyo	Lomas	lom

First Names with Codes

Name	Code	Name	Code	Name	Code	Name	Code
Lona	leo	Lovenah	lav	Luisa	lew	Macdonald	mcd
Lonnie	alp	Lovet	lol	Luke	luc	Mace	tho
Lonsdale	lon	Lovett	lol	Lula	lew	Macey	tho
Lora	lau	Loveviner	lav	Lulie	lew	Mack	mcd
Loraine	loa	Lovey	lol	Lulu	lew	Madaline	mad
Lorances	lau	Lovie	lol	Lumley	lum	Madalyn	mad
Lorane	loa	Lovina	lav	Lumly	lum	Made	mat
Lorayne	loa	Lovinia	lav	Luna	elu	Madelain	mad
Lord	lro	Lovis	lew	Luned	elu	Madelene	mad
Loreen	lau	Low	lau	Lupton	lup	Madelina	mad
Loren	lau	Lowday	lov	Lusia	luc	Madeline	mad
Lorena	lau	Lowe	lau	Lusy	luc	Maden	mad
Lorenzo	lau	Lowis	lew	Lusye	luc	Madge	mar
Loretta	lau	Lowrance	lau	Luther	lut	Madie	may
Lori	lau	Lowrence	lau	Lyall	lya	Madilyn	mad
Lorin	lau	Lowry	low	Lyd	lyd	Madlen	mad
Lorinda	lau	Loyd	llo	Lyda	lyd	Madlin	mad
Loris	lau	Lucas	luc	Lyddia	lyd	Madline	mad
Lorn	lor	Lucaser	luc	Lydea	lyd	Madlyn	mad
Lorna	lor	Lucasta	luc	Lydeah	lyd	Madoc	mao
Lorne	lor	Luce	luc	Lydia	lyd	Madog	mao
Lorraine	loa	Lucetta	luc	Lydiah	lyd	Mady	mad
Lorrane	loa	Lucette	luc	Lyla	lel	Mae	may
Lorrayne	loa	Lucey	luc	Lyn	lyn	Maeve	mva
Lorrie	lau	Lucia	luc	Lynda	lyn	Mag	mar
Lot	lot	Lucian	luc	Lyndon	lyo	Magaden	mad
Lotitia	cha	Lucie	luc	Lyndsay	lid	Magaret	mar
Lottie	cha	Lucien	luc	Lyndsey	lid	Magda	mad
Lotty	cha	Lucile	luc	Lynette	lyn	Magdalan	mad
Lou	lew	Lucilla	luc	Lynn	lyn	Magdalane	mad
Louella	lew	Lucille	luc	Lynne	lyn	Magdalen	mad
Louesa	lew	Lucina	luc	Lynnette	lyn	Magdalena	mad
Louesia	lew	Lucinda	luc	Lynsey	lid	Magdalene	mad
Louezia	lew	Lucius	luc	Lynsie	lid	Magdaline	mad
Louie	lew	Luck	luc	Lynton	lit	Magdallen	mad
Louis	lew	Luckie	luc	Lynwen	lyw	Magdolon	mad
Louisa	lew	Lucrece	lur	Lynwyn	lyw	Mage	mar
Louise	lew	Lucrelia	lur	Lyon	leo	Mageria	mar
Louisia	lew	Lucretia	lur	Lyonel	leo	Magertt	mar
Louiza	lew	Lucy	luc	Lyonell	leo	Magery	mar
Lous	lew	Lucye	luc	Lyra	lyr	Magge	mar
Lousa	lew	Ludovic	lod	Lyss	uly	Maggie	mar
Louse	lew	Ludovick	lod	Lyulf	lyu	Maggy	mar
Lousea	lew	Ludwig	lod	Mab	aml	Magnes	mag
Lousia	lew	Lueiza	lew	Mabel	aml	Magnus	mag
Love	lol	Lueretia	lur	Mabell	aml	Magot	mar
Loveday	lov	Luesa	lew	Mabella	aml	Magret	mar
Lovedy	lov	Luesea	lew	Mabelle	aml	Magt	mar
Lovel	lol	Lueza	lew	Mable	aml	Mahala	mha
Lovell	lol	Luis	lew	Mabyn	mva	Mahalah	mha

Mahalahah	mha	Manfred	man	Margaret	mar	Margreta	mar
Mahalar	mha	Manius	mag	Margareta	mar	Margrete	mar
Mahaler	mha	Manley	mnl	Margaretae	mar	Margrett	mar
Mahalia	mha	Manny	ema	Margaretam	mar	Margretta	mar
Mahela	mha	Manoah	mno	Margarete	mar	Margrette	mar
Mahelea	mha	Manon	may	Margarett	mar	Margrey	mar
Mahlah	mha	Mansel	mna	Margaretta	mar	Margrit	mar
Maidie	mar	Mansell	mna	Margarette	mar	Margrot	mar
Maidline	mad	Mansfield	maf	Margarey	mar	Margrt	mar
Maili	may	Manuel	ema	Margarie	mar	Margry	mar
Maille	may	Manus	mag	Margarit	mar	Margt	mar
Mair	may	Manyus	mag	Margaritae	mar	Marguarita	mar
Maira	may	Mar	mar	Margarite	mar	Marguerite	mar
Mairan	may	Mara	daa	Margarrit	mar	Mari	may
Maire	may	Marabel	mib	Margart	mar	Maria	may
Mairead	mar	Marable	mib	Margary	mar	Mariabella	may
Mairi	may	Marah	daa	Margat	mar	Mariae	may
Mairwen	may	Marai	may	Margatt	mar	Mariah	may
Maisie	mar	Maralyn	may	Marge	mar	Mariam	may
Maisy	mar	Maranda	mir	Marger	mar	Mariame	may
Maitland	mit	Maraquitta	daa	Margerat	mar	Marian	may
Maizy	mar	Maray	may	Margere	mar	Mariana	may
Major	maj	Marbella	mib	Margeret	mar	Mariane	may
Majorie	mar	Marc	mac	Margerett	mar	Mariann	may
Majory	mar	Marcell	mac	Margeria	mar	Marianna	may
Mal	mal	Marcella	mac	Margerie	mar	Marianne	may
Malachi	mah	Marcellus	mac	Margeritt	mar	Marice	mau
Malachy	mah	Marcena	mac	Margerrit	mar	Marie	may
Malacky	mah	Marcene	mac	Margert	mar	Mariel	may
Malaha	mha	Marcha	mac	Margery	mar	Marietta	may
Malcolm	mal	Marci	mac	Margerye	mar	Mariette	may
Malcolme	mal	Marcia	mac	Marget	mar	Marigold	mri
Malcom	mal	Marcie	mac	Margett	mar	Marih	may
Maldwyn	bal	Marcilyn	mac	Margha	mar	Marilyn	may
Malin	mel	Marcina	mac	Margharita	mar	Marin	may
Malina	mel	Marcine	mac	Margiad	mar	Marina	maa
Malinda	mel	Marcius	mac	Margie	mar	Marinda	may
Malkin	mal	Marcus	mac	Margit	mar	Marine	maa
Mall	may	Marcy	mac	Margo	mar	Marion	may
Malley	may	Marduke	mam	Margorie	mar	Marione	may
Mally	may	Marena	maa	Margory	mar	Marionica	may
Malvina	men	Maretta	may	Margot	mar	Mariot	may
Maly	may	Marey	may	Margraet	mar	Marioun	may
Mamie	may	Marg	mar	Margrat	mar	Marious	may
Manard	myn	Margae	mar	Margrate	mar	Maris	may
Manasseh	mas	Margaet	mar	Margreat	mar	Marisa	may
Manda	ama	Margain	mog	Margreate	mar	Marita	may
Mandi	ama	Margar	mar	Margreatt	mar	Marius	may
Mandie	ama	Margarat	mar	Margreit	mar	Marjary	mar
Mandy	ama	Margareet	mar	Margret	mar	Marjery	mar

First Names with Codes

Name	Code	Name	Code	Name	Code	Name	Code
Marjorie	mar	Marte	mrh	Mathewe	maw	May	may
Marjory	mar	Marten	mai	Mathias	maw	Maybel	aml
Mark	mac	Marth	mrh	Mathilda	mat	Maybelle	aml
Marke	mac	Martha	mrh	Matild	mat	Maye	may
Markham	mac	Marthar	mrh	Matilda	mat	Maynard	myn
Marla	mae	Marthay	mrh	Matilday	mat	Mayrie	may
Marleen	mae	Marthe	mrh	Matildia	mat	Maysie	mar
Marlena	mae	Marther	mrh	Matt	mat	Mazala	miz
Marlene	mae	Marthia	mrh	Mattey	mat	Mazella	miz
Marlin	mae	Martho	mrh	Matth	maw	Mazey	mar
Marllia	may	Marthy	mrh	Matthaei	maw	Mazie	mar
Marlton	mla	Marti	mrh	Mattheus	maw	Mazila	miz
Marlyn	mae	Martin	mai	Matthew	maw	Mcdonald	mcd
Marmaducem	mam	Martina	mai	Matthews	maw	Mearcy	mer
Marmaduke	mam	Martine	mai	Matthias	maw	Mearsey	mer
Marna	maa	Martinus	mai	Matthw	maw	Mearye	may
Marnie	maa	Marty	mai	Mattie	mat	Meave	aml
Marolyn	may	Martyn	mai	Mattilda	mat	Mechel	mic
Maron	may	Marvellous	mrv	Mattw	maw	Medora	med
Marria	may	Marvin	mev	Matty	mat	Meg	mar
Marriah	may	Marvyn	mev	Matw	mat	Megan	mar
Marriam	may	Mary	may	Maty	mat	Meggie	mar
Marriame	may	Marya	may	Maud	mat	Mehala	mha
Marrian	may	Maryan	may	Maude	mat	Mehalah	mha
Marriana	may	Maryann	may	Maudlan	mad	Mehalia	mha
Marriane	may	Maryanna	may	Maudland	mad	Mehetabel	meh
Marriann	may	Maryanne	may	Maudlin	mad	Meirion	mii
Marrianna	may	Marye	may	Maudlyn	mad	Mel	men
Marrianne	may	Maryjane	may	Maulde	mat	Melaine	mel
Marrie	may	Marylyn	may	Maura	may	Melanie	mel
Marriea	may	Maryon	may	Maureen	may	Melbourne	meb
Marrien	may	Masella	miz	Maurice	mau	Melcher	mec
Marrin	may	Masie	mar	Maven	mva	Melchior	mec
Marrion	may	Mason	msa	Mavies	mav	Meldred	mid
Marron	may	Massey	mar	Mavin	mva	Melena	emm
Marry	may	Massia	mar	Mavis	mav	Melesina	mil
Marsail	mar	Massie	mar	Mavon	mva	Meleta	mil
Marsaili	mar	Massy	mar	Mawd	mat	Melia	emm
Marsden	mrs	Masy	mar	Mawde	mat	Melias	emm
Marsella	mac	Mat	mat	Mawdeland	mad	Melicent	mil
Marsh	mac	Math	maw	Mawrica	mau	Melina	emm
Marsha	mac	Matha	maw	Mawson	mau	Melinda	mel
Marshal	mra	Mathaei	maw	Max	max	Melior	mli
Marshall	mra	Mathaeus	maw	Maxena	max	Meliora	mli
Marshel	mra	Mathar	maw	Maxene	max	Melissa	mil
Marson	msa	Mathei	maw	Maxime	max	Melita	mil
Marston	mrt	Mather	maw	Maximilian	max	Melitta	mil
Mart	mrh	Mathes	maw	Maxina	max	Mella	may
Martaine	mai	Matheus	maw	Maxine	max	Mellanie	mel
Martainn	mai	Mathew	maw	Maxwell	max	Mellear	mli

Mellicent	mil	Merlin	mev	Michele	mic	Milonis	mie
Mellie	mil	Merlyn	mev	Michell	mic	Milson	mie
Mellissa	mil	Merrick	mau	Michelle	mic	Milton	mie
Melloney	mel	Merridith	mee	Michiel	mic	Mima	jam
Mellony	mel	Merriel	mur	Michl	mic	Mimi	may
Melody	meo	Merril	mur	Mick	mic	Mina	wil
Melonie	mel	Merrion	mii	Mickell	mic	Minadab	wil
Melony	mel	Merry	mee	Mickie	mic	Minella	wil
Melusine	mil	Merton	mro	Micky	mic	Minerva	min
Melva	men	Merville	mrl	Micl	mic	Minette	wil
Melville	mei	Mervin	mev	Middleton	mio	Minie	wil
Melvin	men	Mervyn	mev	Midgely	miy	Minna	wil
Melvina	men	Meryl	mur	Midgley	miy	Minnie	wil
Melvyn	men	Mesella	miz	Miel	mic	Minty	mey
Melyear	mli	Meshach	mes	Mighel	mic	Mira	mir
Melyor	mli	Messella	miz	Mignon	mig	Mirabel	mib
Mendham	mem	Meta	mar	Mignonette	mig	Mirabella	mib
Mennie	may	Methilda	mat	Mihel	mic	Mirah	mir
Menty	mey	Methuselah	met	Mike	mic	Miram	mir
Menzies	mez	Metilda	mat	Milborough	mid	Mirana	mir
Merab	mea	Meuric	mau	Milbrough	mid	Miranda	mir
Meral	mur	Meurig	mau	Milburh	mid	Miria	may
Merall	mur	Meyrick	mau	Milbury	mid	Miriah	may
Meraud	esa	Mezillah	miz	Milca	mia	Miriam	may
Mercedes	mer	Mgaret	mar	Milcah	mia	Mirian	may
Mercer	mer	Mgerye	mar	Mildred	mid	Mirra	mir
Mercey	mer	Mgrett	mar	Mile	mie	Mirran	may
Mercia	mer	Mgt	mar	Milena	mie	Mirren	may
Mercier	mer	Mgy	mar	Miles	mie	Mirriam	may
Mercy	mer	Mhairi	may	Milesa	mie	Missy	mil
Mercye	mer	Mhari	may	Milicent	mil	Mitchel	mic
Meredith	mee	Mia	may	Milison	mil	Mitchell	mic
Merel	mur	Miah	may	Millar	mll	Mitilda	mat
Merfin	mev	Mial	mic	Millbourn	mid	Mitzi	may
Mergeria	mar	Mic	mic	Mille	mil	Mizela	miz
Mergrett	mar	Micaell	mic	Millecent	mil	Mizelle	miz
Meria	may	Micah	mic	Millecente	mil	Moade	mat
Meriah	may	Micahel	mic	Miller	mll	Modesty	moe
Meriam	may	Micaiah	mic	Millesent	mil	Mog	mar
Meribah	may	Mical	mic	Milleson	mil	Moggy	mar
Meridith	mee	Michael	mic	Milley	mil	Moira	may
Merie	mee	Michaela	mic	Millicent	mil	Moire	may
Meriel	mur	Michaelis	mic	Millicenth	mil	Moll	may
Merilyn	mur	Michaell	mic	Millicentiae	mil	Mollie	may
Merina	maa	Michal	mic	Millie	mil	Molly	may
Meriol	mur	Michall	mic	Millison	mil	Mona	mon
Merion	mii	Micheal	mic	Mills	mie	Monday	mod
Merjorie	mar	Micheall	mic	Milly	mil	Monia	mon
Merle	mre	Micheil	mic	Milner	mln	Monica	mon
Merlene	mev	Michel	mic	Milon	mie	Monro	muo

First Names with Codes

Name	Code	Name	Code	Name	Code	Name	Code
Montague	mot	Murdoch	mud	Nany	ann	Nem	neh
Monty	mot	Mureen	may	Naomi	nao	Nemiah	neh
Moor	moo	Muriel	mur	Naomia	nao	Nemiath	neh
Moore	moo	Murray	mua	Naomie	nao	Neomi	nao
Mor	sar	Murrell	mur	Nap	nap	Neptune	ncp
Morag	sar	Murry	mua	Napoleon	nap	Nerida	ned
Moray	mua	Murtagh	mud	Napthali	nah	Nerina	ned
Mordecai	mor	Murtha	mrh	Narcissus	nar	Nerissa	ned
Morden	mog	My	may	Naseem	nas	Nerys	ner
Mordicai	mor	Myel	mic	Nasham	nat	Nessa	van
Moreen	may	Myell	mic	Nasmith	nay	Nessie	agn
Morey	mua	Myer	mye	Nat	nat	Nest	agn
Morfudd	mof	Myers	mye	Natache	nal	Nesta	agn
Morfydd	mof	Myfanwy	fra	Natalia	nal	Neta	agn
Morgan	mog	Mygell	mic	Natalie	nal	Netta	agn
Moria	may	Myghell	mic	Natasha	nal	Nettie	agn
Moriah	may	Myles	mie	Natelie	nal	Netty	hen
Moriarty	moi	Myller	mic	Nath	nat	Neva	nea
Morice	mau	Myra	mir	Natha	nat	Nevan	niv
Morie	mau	Myria	may	Nathalie	nal	Nevell	nev
Morina	maa	Myriam	may	Nathan	nat	Neves	niv
Moris	mau	Myrna	mrn	Nathanael	nat	Nevil	nev
Morley	mol	Myron	mir	Nathaneell	nat	Nevile	nev
Morly	mol	Myrtilla	myt	Nathanel	nat	Nevill	nev
Morna	mrn	Myrtle	myt	Nathanial	nat	Neville	nev
Morris	mau	Mysie	mar	Nathaniel	nat	Nevin	niv
Morry	mau	Myzel	miz	Nathaniell	nat	Nevis	niv
Mortimer	mom	Nab	abr	Nathanil	nat	Newby	neb
Morton	mos	Naboth	nab	Nathanl	nat	Newel	noe
Morven	mov	Nada	nad	Nathl	nat	Newell	noe
Morwenna	mow	Nadene	nad	Natty	nal	Newman	new
Mose	mos	Nadia	nad	Nayland	naa	Newton	net
Moses	mos	Nadine	nad	Naysmith	nay	Niall	nei
Moss	mos	Nadyn	nad	Neal	nei	Nic	nic
Mosses	mos	Nahum	nam	Ned	edw	Nichalos	nic
Mountague	mot	Nail	nei	Neddy	edw	Nichelas	nic
Moureen	may	Naismith	nay	Neh	neh	Nichol	nic
Moy	may	Nan	ann	Nehemiah	neh	Nicholas	nic
Moyes	mos	Nance	ann	Neil	nei	Nicholaus	nic
Moyna	mon	Nancey	ann	Neill	nei	Nicholson	nic
Moyra	may	Nancy	ann	Neilson	nei	Nichs	nic
Moyse	mos	Nanette	ann	Nel	nei	Nick	nic
Mozes	mos	Naney	ann	Nele	nei	Nickallus	nic
Mrgaret	mar	Nanie	ann	Nell	hel	Nickola	nic
Muir	mui	Nanis	ann	Nella	fen	Nickolas	nic
Munga	mun	Nann	ann	Nelley	hel	Nicodemas	nic
Mungo	mun	Nanney	ann	Nellie	hel	Nicol	nic
Munro	muo	Nannie	ann	Nellon	hel	Nicola	nic
Murchadh	mud	Nanny	ann	Nelly	hel	Nicolas	nic
Murdo	mud	Nans	ann	Nelson	nei	Nicolaus	nic

Nicole	nic	Nottingham	not	Omfray	hum	Osweld	osw
Nicolet	nic	Nowel	noe	Oner	hel	Oswell	osw
Nicolette	nic	Nuala	fen	Oonagh	win	Oswin	osi
Nicoya	nic	Nycholas	nic	Ophelia	oph	Oswold	osw
Niel	nei	Nycolas	nic	Orah	dor	Osyth	osc
Nielson	nei	Nycolis	nic	Oralia	aur	Othi	odo
Nigal	nei	Nydia	nad	Oran	orn	Otho	odo
Nigel	nei	Nye	ane	Oren	orn	Oti	odo
Nikola	nic	Nynia	nin	Oriana	ori	Otis	odo
Nilsen	nei	Nyrene	ane	Oriel	aur	Ottilia	odo
Nimrod	nim	Oates	oat	Original	org	Otto	odo
Nina	ann	Obadiah	oba	Orin	orn	Ouida	lew
Nineon	nin	Obed	oba	Orinda	orn	Owain	ewe
Ninia	nin	Obediah	oba	Orla	orl	Owen	ewe
Ninian	nin	Obedience	obe	Orlagh	orl	Owena	ewe
Nita	ann	Oberon	aub	Orlando	rol	Owin	ewe
Niven	niv	Obidiah	oba	Ormerod	orm	Ozzy	osc
Nivian	niv	Ocean	oce	Ormond	oro	Pacience	pai
Noah	noa	Octavia	oct	Ormrod	orm	Packy	pat
Nob	rob	Octavious	oct	Orpah	orp	Pad	pat
Nobby	rob	Octavius	oct	Orpha	orp	Paddy	pat
Noble	nob	Octavus	oct	Orphy	orp	Padraig	pat
Nocolas	nic	Odette	odo	Orrin	orn	Pagan	pag
Noel	noe	Odille	odo	Orris	hor	Page	pae
Noella	noe	Odo	odo	Orry	hor	Paget	pae
Noelle	noe	Odwin	edw	Orson	ors	Paige	pae
Nola	oli	Offy	thp	Orval	orv	Paitence	pai
Nolan	nol	Ogden	ogd	Orville	orv	Palina	pau
Nolen	nol	Ogier	edg	Orwell	orv	Pallison	may
Noll	oli	Oighrig	eup	Osanna	hos	Pally	may
Nollie	oli	Olaf	ola	Osbert	alb	Palmer	pal
Nona	non	Olave	ola	Osborn	osb	Pam	pam
Nonie	hel	Olga	heg	Osborne	osb	Pamala	pam
Nora	hel	Oliff	oli	Osbourne	osb	Pamela	pam
Norah	hel	Oliffe	oli	Osburne	osb	Pamelia	pam
Norbut	nou	Olinda	oln	Oscar	osc	Pamila	pam
Noreen	hel	Oliva	oli	Oscilla	osc	Pamilia	pam
Norfold	nor	Olive	oli	Osgar	osc	Pamilla	pam
Norice	nor	Oliver	oli	Osias	osc	Pammy	pam
Noris	nor	Olivette	oli	Osman	osm	Pansy	pan
Norma	nor	Olivia	oli	Osmond	osm	Paris	pat
Norman	nor	Ollett	oli	Osmund	osm	Park	par
Norna	nor	Ollie	oli	Ossie	osc	Parker	par
Norreys	nor	Olliver	oli	Osston	aug	Parnel	pet
Norrie	nor	Olwen	alw	Ostan	aug	Parnell	pet
Norris	nor	Olwyn	alw	Osten	aug	Parry	har
Norriss	nor	Olympia	oly	Ostin	aug	Parthena	pah
Norton	nor	Olympias	oly	Oston	aug	Parthenia	pah
Norval	nov	Omar	oma	Oswald	osw	Parthina	pah
Norville	nov	Omega	ome	Oswall	osw	Parthine	pah

First Names with Codes

Partick	pat	Peggey	mar	Petty	mat	Phillipe	phi
Partrick	pat	Peggie	mar	Petula	peu	Phillipp	phi
Pascel	pas	Peggotty	mar	Peyton	pey	Phillippa	phi
Pascoe	pas	Peggy	mar	Phabe	phe	Phillis	phy
Pask	pas	Peigi	mar	Phaebe	phe	Phills	phy
Pat	pat	Peirce	pet	Phanah	fra	Phillup	phi
Patarick	pat	Pelham	pel	Pharaoh	pha	Philly	phi
Paterick	pat	Pen	pen	Pharoah	pha	Phillys	phy
Paterson	pat	Penelly	pen	Pheabe	phe	Philomena	pho
Pathania	pah	Penelope	pen	Pheaby	phe	Philpot	phi
Pathena	pah	Peninnah	pen	Pheba	phe	Phineas	phn
Pathenia	pah	Penny	pen	Phebe	phe	Phinehas	phn
Pathina	pah	Penry	har	Phebey	phe	Phob	phe
Patiance	pai	Pentecost	pec	Pheboe	phe	Phobe	phe
Patience	pai	Perceval	per	Pheby	phe	Phoby	phe
Patient	pai	Perceyvall	per	Pheebe	phe	Phoeba	phe
Patientia	pai	Perchance	peh	Pheeby	phe	Phoebe	phe
Patk	pat	Percival	per	Phelim	phy	Phoebea	phe
Patrek	pat	Percivall	per	Phelise	phy	Phoebey	phe
Patric	pat	Percy	per	Phelyp	phi	Phoebia	phe
Patricia	pat	Percyvall	per	Phemie	eup	Phoeby	phe
Patrick	pat	Percywall	per	Pheobe	phe	Phylis	phy
Patrik	pat	Perdita	ped	Pheoby	phe	Phyllis	phy
Patrike	pat	Peregrine	pee	Phiebe	phe	Phythian	viv
Patsy	pat	Perina	pet	Phil	phi	Pia	pia
Patt	pat	Perkin	pet	Phila	phi	Pickles	pic
Pattie	pat	Perl	mar	Philadelphia	dep	Pierce	pet
Patty	pat	Pernel	pet	Philamon	pho	Piercy	pet
Paul	pau	Peronelle	pet	Philander	phl	Pierre	pet
Paula	pau	Perpetua	pep	Philbert	phi	Piers	pet
Pauleen	pau	Perring	pee	Philby	phi	Pip	phi
Paulette	pau	Perry	pee	Philemon	pho	Pippa	phi
Paulina	pau	Persilla	prs	Philibert	phi	Piran	pet
Pauline	pau	Persis	pes	Philidelphia	dep	Plato	plt
Paull	pau	Pery	pee	Philimon	pho	Plaxy	pla
Paulus	pau	Pet	peu	Philip	phi	Pleasance	ple
Pawell	pau	Peta	pet	Philipa	phi	Pleasant	ple
Pawl	pau	Pete	pet	Philipe	phi	Pog	mar
Pawle	pau	Peter	pet	Philiph	phi	Poggy	mar
Paxton	pax	Petere	pet	Philipinna	phi	Pol	pau
Payn	pag	Peternel	pet	Philipp	phi	Polina	may
Peace	pea	Petra	pet	Philippa	phi	Polley	may
Peadair	pet	Petre	pet	Philippus	phi	Polly	may
Pearl	mar	Petri	pet	Philis	phy	Pollyanna	may
Pearse	pet	Petria	pet	Phillapa	phi	Poppy	pop
Pearson	pet	Petrice	pet	Philles	phy	Porter	por
Peater	pet	Petronella	pet	Phillida	phy	Portholan	bat
Peder	pet	Petrus	pet	Phillidelphia	dep	Portia	pot
Peeter	pet	Petter	pet	Phillip	phi	Posthumus	pos
Peg	mar	Pettor	pet	Phillipa	phi	Potter	pet

Pov	pov	Queen	qun	Ralfe	ral	Rea	rhe
Povah	pov	Queenie	qun	Ralph	ral	Reachal	rac
Precila	prs	Quenild	gun	Ralphe	ral	Reachel	rac
Precilla	prs	Quentin	que	Ralphie	ral	Read	rea
Precious	pei	Quincy	que	Ralphina	ral	Reamonn	ray
Prescilla	prs	Quinn	que	Ralston	ras	Reb	reb
Preston	pre	Quintin	que	Ramona	ray	Reba	reb
Price	rhy	Quinton	que	Ramond	ray	Rebacca	reb
Pricella	prs	Rab	rob	Ramsay	rma	Rebackah	reb
Pricila	prs	Rabbie	rob	Ramsden	ram	Rebbeca	reb
Pricilla	prs	Rabi	rob	Ramsey	rma	Rebbecca	reb
Priestley	prt	Rabina	rob	Ranald	reg	Rebbie	reb
Primrose	pri	Raby	rob	Rand	ran	Rebe	reb
Primula	pri	Racey	rac	Randal	ran	Rebeca	reb
Prince	prc	Rachael	rac	Randall	ran	Rebecah	reb
Princess	prc	Rachal	rac	Randel	ran	Rebecay	reb
Prisca	prs	Rachall	rac	Randell	ran	Rebecca	reb
Priscella	prs	Racheal	rac	Randey	ran	Rebeccah	reb
Priscila	prs	Rachel	rac	Randle	ran	Rebecha	reb
Priscilla	prs	Rachele	rac	Randol	ran	Rebecka	reb
Priscillia	prs	Rachell	rac	Randolph	ran	Rebeckah	reb
Prisila	prs	Racherl	rac	Randulphus	ran	Rebeckey	reb
Prisilla	prs	Rachil	rac	Randy	ran	Rebeka	reb
Prissie	prs	Rachill	rac	Ransome	ran	Rebekah	reb
Prissila	prs	Rachl	rac	Ranulf	ran	Rebekkah	reb
Prissilla	prs	Rachle	rac	Raonaid	rac	Reby	reb
Prissillo	prs	Radcliff	rai	Raoul	ral	Recca	reb
Prissulla	prs	Radegon	rad	Raph	ral	Rechel	rac
Prisulla	prs	Radegund	rad	Raphael	rap	Redmond	ray
Protasia	pro	Radford	raf	Raphaela	rap	Redvers	red
Prothesa	pro	Radigall	rad	Raphe	ral	Reece	rhy
Providence	prv	Radolph	ral	Raquel	rac	Reed	rea
Pru	pru	Radolphe	ral	Ratchel	rac	Reenie	ire
Prudance	pru	Radolphus	ral	Ratchell	rac	Rees	rhy
Prudce	pru	Radulphi	ral	Ratcliffe	rat	Reese	rhy
Prudence	pru	Radulphus	ral	Rauf	ral	Reeve	ree
Prudens	pru	Rae	rac	Rauffe	ral	Reeves	ree
Prudhence	pru	Raewyn	row	Raul	ral	Reg	reg
Prudie	pru	Rafael	rap	Raven	rob	Reggie	reg
Prue	pru	Rafe	ral	Rawdon	raw	Regina	reg
Prunella	prn	Raff	ral	Rawling	rol	Reginald	reg
Pryce	rhy	Raffe	ral	Rawson	rol	Regnold	reg
Pter	pet	Raghnall	reg	Ray	ray	Reid	rea
Ptomely	pto	Raibeart	rob	Rayfe	ral	Reighnolde	reg
Pure	pur	Raine	reg	Raymond	ray	Reine	qun
Purina	pur	Raiph	ral	Raymonde	ray	Rejoice	rej
Purly	mar	Raiphe	ral	Raymund	ray	Rejoyce	rej
Purnella	prn	Ralchel	rac	Rayner	reg	Rena	ire
Pyrs	pet	Raleigh	rae	Rbt	rob	Renate	ire
Pyttar	pet	Ralf	ral	Rchard	ric	Rene	ire

First Names with Codes

Name	Code	Name	Code	Name	Code	Name	Code
Renee	ire	Richardson	ric	Roberta	rob	Roisin	ros
Renfred	ren	Richardus	ric	Roberte	rob	Rojer	rog
Renfry	ren	Richd	ric	Roberti	rob	Roland	rol
Renie	ire	Richdus	ric	Robertina	rob	Rolande	rol
Rennie	ire	Richeard	ric	Roberts	rob	Rolf	ral
Repent	rep	Richel	rac	Robertson	rob	Rolla	rol
Reta	mar	Richenda	ric	Robertt	rob	Rolland	rol
Reuben	reu	Richerd	ric	Robertus	rob	Rollo	ral
Reubena	reu	Richi	ric	Robet	rob	Rolly	rol
Reubin	reu	Richie	ric	Robin	rob	Rolph	ral
Reubon	reu	Richmal	ric	Robina	rob	Roma	rom
Reupen	reu	Richmond	ric	Robinetta	rob	Romaine	rom
Reuven	reu	Richoard	ric	Robinson	rob	Romeo	rom
Rex	reg	Richrd	ric	Robr	rob	Romola	rom
Reynard	reg	Richus	ric	Robrt	rob	Ron	reg
Reynaud	reg	Rici	ric	Robson	rob	Rona	row
Reynold	reg	Rick	ric	Robt	rob	Ronald	reg
Rhea	rhe	Ricket	ric	Robte	rob	Rondle	reg
Rheuben	reu	Rickey	ric	Robti	rob	Ronnie	reg
Rhian	rhi	Rickie	fre	Robtus	rob	Rory	roe
Rhiannon	rhi	Ricky	ric	Robyn	rob	Rosa	ros
Rhoada	rho	Ricus	ric	Rocco	roc	Rosabel	ros
Rhoades	rho	Ridlay	rid	Rochelle	roc	Rosabell	ros
Rhoda	rho	Ridley	rid	Rock	roc	Rosaleen	ros
Rhodah	rho	Ridly	rid	Rocky	roc	Rosalia	ros
Rhode	rho	Rigby	rig	Rod	rod	Rosalie	ros
Rhodes	rho	Rika	fre	Roda	rho	Rosalina	ros
Rhody	rho	Riley	ril	Roddie	roe	Rosalind	ros
Rhona	row	Rina	kat	Roddy	roe	Rosalinda	ros
Rhonda	rhn	Ripley	rip	Rode	rho	Rosaline	ros
Rhonwen	row	Rispah	riz	Roderic	roe	Rosalyn	ros
Rhuben	reu	Rita	mar	Roderick	roe	Rosamond	ros
Rhys	rhy	Ritchard	ric	Rodger	rog	Rosamund	ros
Ri	ric	Ritchie	ric	Rodha	rho	Rosan	ros
Ria	rhe	Rizpah	riz	Rodk	roe	Rosana	ros
Ric	ric	Ro	rob	Rodney	rod	Rosanah	ros
Rica	fre	Roald	roa	Rodolph	ral	Rosanan	ros
Ricard	ric	Roanne	ros	Rodolphus	ral	Rosann	ros
Ricardi	ric	Roas	ros	Rodrick	roe	Rosanna	ros
Ricardo	ric	Rob	rob	Rodulph	ral	Rosannae	ros
Ricardus	ric	Robart	rob	Rody	roe	Rosannah	ros
Ricd	ric	Robarte	rob	Rogar	rog	Rose	ros
Rice	rhy	Robartie	rob	Rogeni	rog	Rosea	ros
Rich	ric	Robartt	rob	Roger	rog	Roseana	ros
Richa	ric	Robbert	rob	Rogeri	rog	Roseand	ros
Richad	ric	Robbie	rob	Rogerii	rog	Roseann	ros
Richanda	ric	Robeart	rob	Rogers	rog	Roseanna	ros
Richard	ric	Robena	rob	Rogher	rog	Roseannah	ros
Richarde	ric	Rober	rob	Rohan	row	Roseanne	ros
Richardi	ric	Robert	rob	Rois	ros	Rosehannah	ros

Name	Code	Name	Code	Name	Code	Name	Code
Roselia	ros	Royston	roy	Sacha	ale	Sanderson	ale
Roselin	ros	Roza	ros	Sacheveral	sac	Sandford	ale
Roseline	ros	Rozalyn	ros	Sadie	sar	Sandra	ale
Rosella	ros	Rozanna	ros	Sadler	sad	Sands	ale
Rosemary	ros	Rozina	ros	Saer	say	Sandy	ale
Rosemond	ros	Ruairidh	roe	Sagar	sga	Sanson	sas
Rosemund	ros	Rube	reu	Saidee	sar	Saphia	sop
Rosena	ros	Ruben	reu	Saint	cyn	Saphira	sap
Rosenia	ros	Rubie	reu	Sal	sar	Sapphira	sap
Roseta	ros	Rubin	reu	Salamon	sol	Sapphire	sap
Rosetta	ros	Rubina	reu	Salathiel	saa	Sar	sar
Rosette	ros	Rubuen	reu	Salena	cel	Sara	sar
Rosey	ros	Ruby	reu	Salina	cel	Sarae	sar
Roshannah	ros	Rubyna	reu	Salla	sar	Saragh	sar
Rosheen	ros	Rudd	ral	Salley	sar	Sarah	sar
Rosie	ros	Rudolf	ral	Sally	sar	Saraha	sar
Rosiland	ros	Rudolph	ral	Salmon	sao	Sarahae	sar
Rosilla	ros	Rudy	ral	Saloma	sol	Sarahan	sar
Rosilyn	ros	Rueben	reu	Salome	sol	Sarahann	sar
Rosimond	ros	Rufe	ruf	Salvador	sav	Sarai	sar
Rosina	ros	Rufus	ruf	Salvator	sav	Saraid	sar
Rosita	ros	Ruiben	reu	Salvatore	sav	Saram	sar
Roslin	ros	Ruiraidh	roe	Saly	sar	Saran	sar
Roslyn	ros	Rupert	rob	Sam	sam	Saranna	sar
Rosomond	ros	Ruperta	rob	Samantha	san	Sarar	sar
Ross	rso	Rurik	roe	Samarie	sam	Saray	sar
Rossalyn	ros	Russ	rus	Samella	sam	Sarayh	sar
Rossella	ros	Russel	rus	Samentha	sam	Sareh	sar
Rosser	ros	Russell	rus	Sameull	sam	Sarena	sar
Rossetta	ros	Rusty	rus	Samewel	sam	Sarey	sar
Rossette	ros	Ruth	rut	Samewell	sam	Sargant	sag
Rosslyn	rso	Ruthe	rut	Saml	sam	Sargeant	sag
Rosy	ros	Ruthie	rut	Samll	sam	Sargent	sag
Rotheric	roe	Ruthven	rut	Sammuel	sam	Sarh	sar
Rowan	row	Ryan	rya	Sammy	sam	Sarha	sar
Rowe	row	Rychard	ric	Sampson	sas	Sariah	sar
Rowena	row	Rycharde	ric	Samson	sas	Sarina	sar
Rowland	rol	Rychardus	ric	Samual	sam	Sarinah	sar
Rowlandson	rol	Rycherd	ric	Samuel	sam	Sarita	sar
Rowley	rwo	Rychert	ric	Samuelis	sam	Sarjeant	sag
Roxana	rox	Sabara	sai	Samuell	sam	Sarjent	sag
Roxie	rox	Sabath	sat	Samuiel	sam	Sarrah	sar
Roy	rob	Sabeeha	sab	Samul	sam	Sary	sar
Royal	ryo	Sabin	sab	Samule	sam	Sarye	sar
Royalyn	ryo	Sabina	sab	Samulel	sam	Sasha	ale
Royce	ros	Sabinah	sab	Samvell	sam	Saul	sau
Royden	ron	Sabine	sab	Samwell	sam	Saunder	ale
Roydon	ron	Sabra	sai	Sanchia	cyn	Saunders	ale
Royle	ryo	Sabrah	sai	Sander	ale	Saundra	ale
Roystan	roy	Sabrina	sai	Sanders	ale	Savil	sva

First Names with Codes

Savile	sva	Selvin	sew	Sharmaine	cae	Sibbilla	sib
Savill	sva	Selwyn	sew	Sharman	cae	Sibby	sib
Savilla	sva	Sena	ase	Sharmane	cae	Sibella	sib
Savina	sab	Sence	cyn	Sharon	shr	Sibley	sib
Sawney	ale	Senga	agn	Sharp	shp	Sibly	sib
Saxon	sax	Seodina	sid	Sharpe	shp	Sibyl	sib
Sayer	say	Seonag	joa	Sharry	shr	Sibylla	sib
Scarlet	sca	Seonaid	joa	Sharyl	cha	Sicil	cec
Scarlett	sca	Seoras	geo	Shaun	joh	Sicila	cec
Scharlotte	cha	Sephen	ste	Shavon	joa	Sicilia	cec
Scholastica	sch	Sepp	jos	Shaw	shw	Sicily	cec
Science	cyn	September	sep	Shawn	joh	Sid	sid
Scilla	prs	Septima	sep	Sheba	bah	Siddy	sid
Scott	sco	Septimas	sep	Sheena	joa	Sidney	sid
Seabra	sai	Septimus	sep	Sheila	cec	Sidonia	sid
Seabright	sbe	Sera	sar	Shelagh	cec	Sidony	sid
Seamark	sey	Serah	sar	Shelah	cec	Sidwell	sdi
Seamor	sey	Seraphina	ser	Shelia	cec	Siegfried	sie
Seamore	sey	Seraphita	ser	Shelley	shi	Sig	sig
Seamour	sey	Serena	seo	Shelly	shi	Sigerith	sir
Seamus	jam	Serenah	seo	Shelton	shl	Sigismund	sig
Sean	joh	Sereno	seo	Shena	joa	Sigmund	sig
Seasaidh	jes	Serenus	seo	Sheona	joa	Signatora	sia
Seasar	caa	Sergeant	sag	Shephard	she	Sigrid	sir
Seaton	sen	Serina	seo	Shepherd	she	Sila	sil
Seb	seb	Serle	see	Sheppard	she	Silas	sil
Seba	seb	Seth	set	Sher	shi	Sile	cec
Sebastian	seb	Seton	sen	Sheralyn	cha	Sileas	sil
Sebell	sib	Seumas	jam	Sherida	shd	Silena	cel
Sebert	sbe	Seumus	jam	Sheridan	shd	Silence	sic
Sebina	sab	Sewal	sea	Sherilyn	cha	Silias	sil
Sebra	sai	Seward	sed	Sheron	shr	Silina	cel
Secilia	cec	Sewell	sea	Sherralyn	cha	Sill	sic
Secundus	sec	Sexa	sex	Sherralynn	cha	Silueness	sil
Seelia	cec	Sextus	sex	Sherry	car	Silva	sil
Sefton	sef	Seymour	sey	Sheryl	cha	Silvanus	sil
Selah	seh	Sezar	caa	Sheumais	jam	Silvas	sil
Selbey	sel	Shackleton	shc	Shevon	joa	Silvenus	sil
Selby	sel	Shadrac	sha	Shirlene	shi	Silvester	sil
Selda	grs	Shadrach	sha	Shirley	shi	Silvey	sil
Sele	cel	Shadrack	sha	Shirly	shi	Silvia	sil
Selena	cel	Shaine	joh	Shiven	joa	Sim	sim
Selestria	cel	Shamus	jam	Sholto	sho	Simean	sim
Selia	cec	Shane	joh	Shudrach	sha	Simeon	sim
Selin	cel	Sharleen	cha	Shurley	shi	Simieon	sim
Selina	cel	Sharlet	cha	Shusan	sus	Simion	sim
Selinah	cel	Sharlot	cha	Shusanna	sus	Simon	sim
Selinda	cel	Sharlott	cha	Sian	joa	Simond	sim
Seline	cel	Sharlotte	cha	Siari	cha	Simonde	sim
Selma	ans	Sharmain	cae	Sib	sib	Simone	sim

Name	Code	Name	Code	Name	Code	Name	Code
Simpson	sim	Stafford	stf	Suannah	sus	Swales	swa
Simund	sim	Stamford	sto	Sudney	sid	Swaley	swa
Sina	joa	Stan	sta	Sue	sus	Swinbourne	swn
Sinclair	sin	Stanby	sta	Sugden	sug	Swinburne	swn
Sindy	luc	Stanford	sto	Suhannah	sus	Swindeniah	swi
Sine	joa	Stanhope	sta	Suke	sus	Swire	swr
Sinead	joa	Stanislas	stn	Sukey	sus	Swithin	swi
Siobahn	joa	Stanley	sta	Sukie	sus	Swithun	swi
Sioban	joa	Stanton	stt	Suky	sus	Sybbell	sib
Siobhan	joa	Staphen	ste	Sullivan	sul	Sybel	sib
Sion	joh	Starkie	stk	Sully	sul	Sybella	sib
Sir	sri	Statia	ana	Sulwen	sew	Sybil	sib
Sirida	sir	Steaphen	ste	Sulwyn	sew	Sybill	sib
Sis	cec	Steaven	ste	Sus	sus	Sydney	sid
Sisley	cec	Steephen	ste	Susa	sus	Sydonah	sid
Sissie	cec	Stefan	ste	Susahnah	sus	Sydonia	sid
Sissy	cec	Stella	est	Susan	sus	Sylvan	sil
Siward	siw	Stepen	ste	Susana	sus	Sylvanus	sil
Sloane	slo	Stephan	ste	Susanae	sus	Sylvester	sil
Smith	smi	Stephana	ste	Susanah	sus	Sylvia	sil
Smyth	smi	Stephane	ste	Susanay	sus	Sylvina	sil
Snowdrop	sno	Stephani	ste	Susand	sus	Sym	sim
Sofia	sop	Stephania	ste	Susaner	sus	Symo	sim
Sol	sol	Stephanie	ste	Susanh	sus	Symon	sim
Solina	cel	Stephanus	ste	Susanha	sus	Symond	sim
Solly	sol	Stephen	ste	Susann	sus	Syndonia	sid
Soloman	sol	Stephenson	ste	Susanna	sus	Syriack	cyi
Solomon	sol	Stepheus	ste	Susannah	sus	Syssely	cec
Somerled	sam	Stephie	ste	Susanne	sus	Sysselye	cec
Sonia	sop	Stephn	ste	Susanney	sus	Syth	set
Sonya	sop	Stepn	ste	Susey	sus	Tabatha	tab
Soph	sop	Sterling	sti	Sush	sus	Tabby	tab
Sopha	sop	Stev	ste	Sushana	sus	Tabetha	tab
Sophi	sop	Steve	ste	Sushanah	sus	Tabez	tab
Sophia	sop	Steven	ste	Sushannah	sus	Tabitha	tab
Sophiah	sop	Stevens	ste	Susie	sus	Tabotha	tab
Sophie	sop	Stevyn	ste	Suson	sus	Tace	sic
Sophy	sop	Stew	stw	Sussan	sus	Tacey	sic
Sopia	sop	Steward	stw	Sussana	sus	Tacye	sic
Soraya	sor	Stewart	stw	Sussanah	sus	Tad	tim
Sorcha	sar	Stifania	ste	Sussanna	sus	Tadhgh	tim
Spash	asp	Stilla	est	Sussannah	sus	Taffy	dav
Spence	spe	Stimpson	stm	Susy	sus	Tagget	agn
Spencer	spe	Stirling	sti	Sutcliffe	sut	Taggy	agn
Spenser	spe	Stodart	std	Suzan	sus	Talbertha	bet
Squire	squ	Stratford	str	Suzana	sus	Talbot	tal
Srah	sar	Stuart	stw	Suzanna	sus	Talitha	tai
Stacey	ana	Suan	sus	Suzannah	sus	Tallulah	tau
Stacie	ana	Suana	sus	Suzanne	sus	Tam	tho
Stacy	ana	Suanh	sus	Swailey	swa	Tamah	tam

Name	Code	Name	Code	Name	Code	Name	Code
Tamar	tam	Terence	ter	Theresa	ter	Thrift	thf
Tamara	tam	Teresa	ter	Theresdi	ter	Ths	tho
Tamaris	daa	Teresia	ter	Therese	ter	Thursa	ter
Tamasin	tho	Teressa	ter	Theriza	ter	Thursey	ter
Tamasine	tho	Tereza	ter	Thermuthis	thr	Thurstan	thu
Tamazine	tho	Terrance	ter	Therna	ter	Thursten	thu
Tamer	tam	Terrence	ter	Theron	thn	Thurston	thu
Tammas	tho	Terrie	tcr	Thersa	ter	Thurza	ter
Tammy	tho	Terry	ter	Thersdi	ter	Thyra	thy
Tamor	tam	Tersia	ter	Therza	ter	Thyrsa	ter
Tamsin	tho	Tertius	tet	Thickell	thk	Thyrza	ter
Tamson	tho	Terza	ter	Thimothy	tim	Tib	eli
Tamyra	tam	Tess	ter	Thimsy	tim	Tibald	the
Tamzen	tho	Tessa	ter	Thirkill	thk	Tibby	eli
Tana	tat	Tesse	ter	Thirsa	ter	Tibia	eli
Tancred	tan	Tessie	ter	Thirza	ter	Tiffany	thp
Tanis	tat	Tetsy	eli	Thirzar	ter	Tilda	mat
Tansy	tas	Tetty	eli	Tho	tho	Tilden	til
Tanya	tat	Teubald	the	Thoams	tho	Till	mat
Tara	tar	Tewdwr	edw	Thoas	tho	Tillah	mat
Tary	oct	Thad	tim	Thom	tho	Tilley	mat
Tasha	nal	Thaddeus	tim	Thoma	tho	Tillie	mat
Tate	tae	Thaddius	tim	Thomae	tho	Tillot	mat
Tatiana	tat	Thalia	thi	Thomalin	tho	Tilly	mat
Tave	oct	Thamar	tam	Thomam	tho	Tilpah	zia
Tavie	oct	Thea	edw	Thomas	tho	Tim	tim
Taylor	tay	Theadosia	edw	Thomasin	tho	Timmy	tim
Tayma	tam	Theaphilus	thp	Thomasina	tho	Timoth	tim
Teague	tim	Thekla	tha	Thomasine	tho	Timothe	tim
Tearlach	cha	Theldred	eth	Thomason	tho	Timotheus	tim
Teasdale	tea	Thelma	thl	Thomat	tho	Timothey	tim
Ted	edw	Theny	pah	Thomazen	tho	Timothia	tim
Tedbald	the	Theo	edw	Thomazin	tho	Timothy	tim
Tedbar	the	Theobald	the	Thomazine	tho	Timy	tim
Teddy	edw	Theodocia	edw	Thome	tho	Tina	chr
Tegwen	teg	Theodora	edw	Thomenia	tho	Tirza	ter
Tegwyn	teg	Theodore	edw	Thomison	tho	Tirzah	ter
Teige	tim	Theodoric	edw	Thomizon	tho	Tish	let
Telford	tel	Theodorus	edw	Thommas	tho	Tissy	eli
Temperance	tem	Theodosia	edw	Thompson	tho	Titty	eli
Temperence	tem	Theoph	thp	Thoms	tho	Titus	tit
Tempest	tee	Theophania	thp	Thomson	tho	Tity	eli
Temple	tep	Theophelus	thp	Thora	thy	Tobe	tob
Tenant	ten	Theophila	thp	Thorkill	thk	Tobiah	tob
Tennant	ten	Theophili	thp	Thorley	toh	Tobias	tob
Tenny	tey	Theophilius	thp	Thornley	toh	Tobin	tob
Tennyson	tey	Theophilus	thp	Thornton	tht	Tobit	tob
Terance	ter	Theophius	thp	Thorold	thd	Toby	tob
Terasa	ter	Theophphelous	thp	Thorston	thu	Todius	edw
Terena	ter	Theoples	thp	Thos	tho	Tolly	bat

Tom	tho	Trish	pat	Uriah	uri	Verena	ver
Tomas	tho	Trissie	bea	Urian	urn	Vergenie	vir
Tomasin	tho	Tristan	trs	Uriel	url	Verita	vei
Tomasine	tho	Tristram	trs	Urien	urn	Verity	vei
Tomenia	tho	Trix	bea	Urina	uri	Verley	vel
Tomey	tho	Trixie	bea	Urith	urh	Verlie	vel
Tomina	tho	Troth	tro	Ursiley	urs	Verna	ven
Tomison	tho	Trothe	tro	Ursula	urs	Verney	ven
Tomlinson	tho	Troy	tor	Urwin	irv	Vernie	ven
Tommina	tho	Trud	get	Uzziah	uzz	Vernon	ven
Tommy	tho	Truda	get	Val	val	Verona	ver
Tommyson	tho	Trudi	get	Valantine	val	Veronica	vcr
Tomsen	tho	Trudie	get	Valarie	val	Vessy	ves
Tomson	tho	Trudy	get	Valatine	val	Vest	ves
Tony	ant	True	tur	Valda	vad	Vesta	ves
Tonya	tat	Truman	tru	Valence	val	Veta	eli
Topsy	top	Tryphena	try	Valencia	val	Vi	vio
Torcall	thk	Tryphoena	try	Valentia	val	Vian	viv
Tormod	nor	Tryphon	try	Valentina	val	Vic	vic
Torold	thd	Tryphosa	try	Valentine	val	Vick	vic
Torquil	thk	Tudor	edw	Valeria	val	Vickers	vic
Tos	tho	Turlough	ter	Valerian	val	Vicky	vic
Tottie	cha	Turner	tun	Valerie	val	Victor	vic
Totty	cha	Turstan	thu	Valma	wil	Victoria	vic
Tracie	ter	Tyler	tyl	Van	van	Victorine	vic
Tracy	ter	Tyra	thy	Vance	vac	Vida	dav
Traiton	trt	Tyrone	tyr	Vancelo	vas	Vidal	via
Travers	tra	Uchtred	uch	Vanda	wan	Viel	via
Travis	tra	Ughtred	uch	Vane	van	Vilma	wil
Trayton	trt	Uileos	uly	Vanessa	van	Vina	lav
Trecesea	ter	Uillean	wil	Vanetta	vee	Vince	vin
Treena	kat	Uisdean	hug	Vanora	gue	Vincent	vin
Trefor	tre	Ulick	uly	Vanslow	vas	Vincentia	vin
Treina	kat	Ulla	urs	Varey	may	Vine	vie
Trena	kat	Ullace	uly	Varie	may	Viney	lav
Trephena	try	Ulric	ulr	Vashti	vah	Vinny	vin
Tresa	ter	Ulrica	ulr	Vasilis	bas	Viola	vio
Treva	tre	Ulysses	uly	Vaughan	vau	Violet	vio
Treveens	tre	Umfray	hum	Veda	dav	Violetta	vio
Trevor	tre	Una	win	Velda	vad	Virgie	vir
Treza	ter	Unice	eun	Velma	wil	Virgil	vig
Tricia	pat	Unis	eun	Venetia	vee	Virgina	vir
Triffie	try	Unity	uni	Vennice	van	Virginia	vir
Trina	kat	Uphemia	eup	Venus	veu	Virtue	vit
Trinetta	kat	Upton	upt	Venyce	van	Vita	vic
Trinita	kat	Urana	ura	Venyse	van	Vitalis	via
Trinity	tri	Urania	ura	Vera	ver	Vivian	viv
Triphena	try	Urban	urb	Verdon	ved	Vivien	viv
Triphosa	try	Urena	uri	Verdun	ved	Vivienne	viv
Tris	bea	Uria	uri	Vere	ver	Voilet	vio

First Names with Codes

Name	Code	Name	Code	Name	Code	Name	Code
Vrsula	urs	Wells	wle	Willia	wil	Winnfred	win
Vyvian	viv	Welmot	wil	William	wil	Winnie	win
Vyvyan	viv	Wendy	wen	Williame	wil	Winnifred	win
Wade	wae	Wenford	wyf	Williamina	wil	Winston	wis
Wain	way	Wenifred	win	Williams	wil	Winthrop	wih
Wainwright	wai	Wenn	win	Williamson	wil	Winton	wis
Wal	wal	Wenny	win	Williamus	wil	Wisdom	wim
Waldeve	wad	Wesley	wes	Willian	wil	Witney	whi
Waldive	wad	Wesly	wes	Willie	wil	Wlliam	wil
Waldo	osw	West	wes	Willielmi	wil	Wm	wil
Walford	waf	Westley	wes	Willielmus	wil	Wolf	wol
Walker	wak	Westly	wes	Willim	wil	Wood	woo
Wallace	waa	Weston	wet	Willimi	wil	Woodrow	woo
Waller	wla	Whalley	waa	Willims	wil	Woodward	woo
Walliam	wil	Whalter	wal	Willimus	wil	Worthey	wor
Wallis	waa	Wharton	wha	Willis	wil	Worthy	wor
Wallter	wal	Wheatley	whe	Willm	wil	Wright	wri
Wally	waa	Whiston	wet	Willmi	wil	Wyat	guy
Walt	wal	Whitmee	whi	Willms	wil	Wybert	wyb
Walter	wal	Whitney	whi	Willmus	wil	Wylie	wil
Walton	wat	Whittaker	wht	Willo	wio	Wylliam	wil
Wanda	wan	Wifred	wlf	Willoby	wio	Wyllm	wil
Wander	gue	Wilbert	wib	Willoughby	wio	Wyllya	wil
Wanita	joa	Wilbur	wib	Wills	wil	Wyndham	wyn
Wannore	gue	Wilby	wib	Willum	wil	Wynethred	win
Wannour	gue	Wilf	wlf	Willus	wil	Wynford	wyf
Ward	wra	Wilford	wif	Willy	wil	Wynne	win
Wareing	wrr	Wilfred	wlf	Willyam	wil	Xan	ale
Warick	waw	Wilfrid	wlf	Wilm	wil	Xanthe	xan
Warin	war	Wilfridi	wlf	Wilma	wil	Xanthippe	xan
Waring	wrr	Wilfridus	wlf	Wilmett	wil	Xavier	xav
Warner	war	Wilhelm	wil	Wilmi	wil	Xaviera	xav
Warren	wrr	Wilhelmi	wil	Wilmit	wil	Xenia	zea
Warton	wha	Wilhelmina	wil	Wilmot	wil	Xopher	chr
Warwick	waw	Wilhelmus	wil	Wilms	wil	Xphofer	chr
Washington	was	Wilhilmina	wil	Wilson	wil	Xpo	chr
Wat	wal	Wiliam	wil	Wilton	wit	Xpofer	chr
Water	wal	Wilkinson	wil	Wilyam	wil	Xpoferi	chr
Waters	wal	Will	wil	Wimifrid	win	Xpoferus	chr
Watkin	wal	Willa	wil	Windsor	wid	Xpoffer	chr
Watson	wal	Willaba	wio	Wineford	win	Xpofferi	chr
Watt	wal	Willaim	wil	Winefred	win	Xpofferus	chr
Watter	wal	Willam	wil	Winey	win	Xtian	chr
Watty	wal	Willeam	wil	Winfred	win	Xto	chr
Wave	wav	Willelmus	wil	Winiford	win	Xtopher	chr
Waverly	wav	Willem	wil	Winifred	win	Xtopheri	chr
Wayne	way	Willfraie	wlf	Winifridae	win	Yalonda	vio
Webster	web	Willhelmina	wil	Winifrith	win	Yancy	yan
Welberry	wee	Willhimina	wil	Winnefrid	win	Yasmin	jan
Wellington	wel	Willi	wil	Winney	win	Yasmina	jan

Yasmine	jan	Zebulen	zeu
Yden	edt	Zebulin	zeu
Yehudi	jud	Zebulon	zeu
Yesbell	eli	Zebulun	zeu
Yestin	jus	Zechariah	zac
Yetta	hen	Zecheriah	zac
Yiesha	aih	Zedekiah	zed
Ynes	agn	Zeke	eze
Yola	vio	Zelda	grs
Yolande	vio	Zelie	azl
Yorath	edw	Zelina	azl
Yorick	yor	Zelinda	cel
Yoruth	edw	Zelma	ans
Young	you	Zena	zea
Yseult	iso	Zenas	zea
Ysolda	iso	Zenda	zea
Ysonde	iso	Zenobia	zen
Yvette	ivo	Zeph	zep
Yvon	ivo	Zephaniah	zep
Yvonne	ivo	Zerrubabel	zer
Yvor	ivr	Zerrubbabel	zer
Ywain	ewe	Zerviah	xav
Zabdiel	zab	Zeta	zit
Zabulon	zeu	Zetta	ros
Zacariah	zac	Zilah	zil
Zacarias	zac	Ziliah	zil
Zacceus	zac	Zilla	zil
Zacchaeus	zac	Zillah	zil
Zaccheus	zac	Zilliah	zil
Zacharia	zac	Zilpah	zia
Zachariah	zac	Zilpha	zia
Zacharias	zac	Zimri	zim
Zachary	zac	Zina	zea
Zack	zac	Ziporah	zip
Zackariah	zac	Zipporah	zip
Zackriah	zac	Ziprah	zip
Zadok	zad	Zita	zit
Zaida	zai	Zoe	zoe
Zak	zac	Zollie	sol
Zake	zac	Zona	zon
Zandra	ale	Zora	sar
Zane	joa	Zsa	sus
Zara	sar	Zuba	azu
Zaria	aza	Zuhra	sar
Zarita	sar	Zuleika	zul
Zavier	xav	Zusi	sus
Zayda	zai	Zylla	zil
Zebadiah	zeb	Zylpha	zia
Zebedee	zeb	Zyprian	cyp
Zebulan	zeu		

Codes giving Variants

Code	Diminutive	Other
aar	Aaras	
	Aaron	
	Aron	
	Arran	
	Arron	
aba	Abia	
	Abiah	
	Abiatha	
	Abiathar	
	Abiel	
	Abijah	
abb	**Abbot**	
abd	**Abednego**	
	Abednegs	
abe	**Abimelech**	
abi	Abagail	abr
	Abagil	
	Abagirl	
	Abaigael	
	Abbey	
	Abbie	
	Abbigal	
	Abbigale	
	Abbigill	
	Abby	
	Abbygale	
	Abegall	
	Abey	
	Abiagail	
	Abie	
	Abig	
	Abigah	
	Abigaiel	
	Abigail	
	Abigaile	
	Abigaill	
	Abigal	
	Abigale	
	Abigall	
	Abigel	
	Abigial	
	Abigiel	
	Abigil	
	Abigill	
	Abygall	
	Gael	
	Gail	
	Gale	
	Gayel	

Code	Diminutive	Other
	Gayle	
abm	**Amber**	
	Ambler	
abn	**Abner**	
	Avner	
	Ebner	
abr	Ab	abi
	Abe	
	Abel	
	Abell	
	Abi	
	Able	
	Abm	
	Abr	
	Abra	
	Abrabham	
	Abrah	
	Abraha	
	Abrahaham	
	Abraham	
	Abrahamina	
	Abrahem	
	Abrahim	
	Abram	
	Abreham	
	Abrh	
	Abrham	
	Abrm	
	Bram	
	Bramley	
	Nab	
abs	Absalam	
	Absalom	
	Abselon	
	Absolam	
	Absolan	
	Absolom	
	Absolon	
abu	**Abderus**	
	Abdyas	
	Abediah	
acc	**Accepted**	
ace	Ace	
	Acelin	
	Acie	
	Ascelina	
ach	Achile	
	Achiles	
	Achillas	
	Achille	

Code	Diminutive	Other
	Achilles	
aci	**Alcina**	
ack	**Ackroyd**	
	Akeroyd	
ada	Ada	air
	Adah	alb
	Adaidh	ali
	Adaiha	del
	Adalade	edt
	Adalaid	eli
	Adalaida	hel
	Adalaide	
	Adaline	
	Adam	
	Adamina	
	Adamus	
	Addelina	
	Addie	
	Addison	
	Addy	
	Ade	
	Adekin	
	Adel	
	Adela	
	Adelade	
	Adelaid	
	Adelaide	
	Adele	
	Adelia	
	Adeliade	
	Adelid	
	Adelide	
	Adelie	
	Adelin	
	Adelina	
	Adeline	
	Adhamh	
	Adilade	
	Adiline	
	Aedyline	
	Aida	
	Alina	
	Aline	
	Eda	
	Edom	
	Heidi	
	Hiedi	
ade	**Aderyn**	
adi	**Adina**	
adl	**Adlai**	

adm	**Admiral**			Anis		ais	**Aisling**	
	Ahmed			Anise			Ashling	
ado	Adolf	dor		Annais		ala	Ailean	alb
	Adolpha			Annas			Al	hel
	Adolphe			Annes			**Alan**	mad
	Adolphus			Annice			Alanna	
	Delphus			Annis			Alano	
	Dolf			Anniss			Alanus	
	Dolphus			Annissa			Aleen	
adr	Adria			Annot			Aleine	
	Adrian			Annys			Alen	
	Adriana			Augnes			Aleyn	
	Adrianne			Egnes			Allan	
	Adriel			Egness			Allane	
	Adrien			Nessie			Allen	
	Adriene			Nest			Allin	
	Adrienne			Nesta			Alyn	
	Hadrian			Neta			Ayleen	
ael	**Aled**			Netta		alb	Abert	ada
aen	Annalie			Nettie			Adalberta	ala
	Annalisa			Senga			Alber	bem
	Annelie			Tagget			**Albert**	bet
	Anneliese			Taggy			Alberta	cut
aet	Aletta			Ynes			Albertine	eth
	Alette		ahm	**Ahmed**			Albright	gil
aga	Agace	agn	aid	Aden			Alperta	phi
	Agatha			Adin			Aubert	wib
agl	Alga			Aed			Bartie	
	Algar			**Aidan**			Bert	
	Alger			Aithne			Bertie	
agn	Aggie	aga		Haddon			Bertina	
	Aggy	ann		Hadyn			Birt	
	Agn	hel		Haydn			Birtie	
	Agnas	joa		Haydon			Birty	
	Agnass	win	aih	Aesha			Burt	
	Agnes			Aiesha			Burton	
	Agness			**Aisha**			Elbertina	
	Agnet			Aisia			Elbright	
	Agneta			Ayesha			Haburd	
	Agnete			Ieashia			Halbert	
	Agnez			Iesha			Harbert	
	Agnis			Yiesha			Harbord	
	Agniss		ail	Almeric			Haribert	
	Agnus			**Almira**			Herbert	
	Agnys		ain	**Ainsley**			Herbertus	
	Anas			Ansley			Herbet	
	Anes		air	Arleen	ada		Herbit	
	Anese			Arlene	cha		Hobart	
	Angnes			**Arline**			Hubbard	
	Anice			Arlyne			Hubert	

	Hurbert			Eck			Ailis
	Osbert			Elexius			Ailison
alc	**Alberic**			Lex			Alace
ald	Alda			Lexi			Alas
	Aldo			Sacha			Alce
	Aldous			Sander			Ales
	Aldred			Sanders			Alese
	Aldreda			Sanderson			Aleson
	Alida			Sandford			Alessone
	Elda			Sandra			Alessoun
	Eldred			Sands			Aley
ale	Alasdair	ali		Sandy			Ali
	Alastair	and		Sasha			Alias
	Alaxander	cas		Saunder			Alic
	Alec			Saunders			**Alice**
	Alester			Saundra			Alicea
	Alex			Sawney			Alicia
	Alexa			Xan			Aliciae
	Alexader			Zandra			Aliciam
	Alexand		alf	Alf	fre		Alicie
	Alexander			Alfd			Alis
	Alexanderina			Alfie			Alisa
	Alexanderus			Alford			Alise
	Alexandra			Alfrd			Alisha
	Alexandria			Alfread			Alisia
	Alexandrina			**Alfred**			Alison
	Alexd			Alfreda			Alisone
	Alexder			Alfredo			Alisoun
	Alexdr			Alfrid			Allas
	Alexeander			Alfried			Alles
	Alexia			Allfred			Alleson
	Alexina			Alured			Allesona
	Alcxine			Alvery			Alless
	Alexis			Avery			Alley
	Alexr			Elfleda			Allice
	Alexsander			Elfreda			Allie
	Alexssaunder			Elfrida			Allis
	Alick			Halfred			Allison
	Alics			Leda			Allse
	Alisdair		alg	**Algernon**			Ally
	Alistair			Algie			Allyson
	Alister			Algy			Alse
	Alixander		alh	**Aldhelm**			Alsie
	Allaster		ali	Adelice	ada		Alucia
	Allex			Adeliza	ale		Aly
	Allexander			Aiison	ele		Alyce
	Allexr			Ailce	eli		Alys
	Alli			Aileson	elj		Alysia
	Allick			Ailidh			Ayles
	Alxr			Ailie			Elice

	Elicia			Alvin			Ama	ism
	Elies			Alvina			**Amabel**	
	Elis			Alvira			Amable	
	Elise			Alwyn			Amas	
	Elison			Alwyna			Amata	
	Elisone			Aylwin			Ame	
	Ellas			Ellwyn			Amee	
	Ellece			Elvin			Amer	
	Elles			Elvina			Amey	
	Elless			Elwina			Amia	
	Ellison			Elwyn			Amiable	
	Elliss			Olwen			Amias	
all	**Allwood**			Olwyn			Amie	
alm	**Alma**		aly	Aloisa	lew		Amies	
aln	Alba	alw		Alowis			Amis	
	Alban			Aloyisia			Amry	
	Albin			Aloysia			Amy	
	Albina			**Aloysius**			Amyas	
	Albinia			Eloisa			Anabella	
	Albion			Eloise			Anaebella	
	Alva			Helewise			Annabel	
	Alvah		ama	Aman	mir		Annabell	
alo	Allon			Amand			Annabella	
alp	Alfonce			**Amanda**			Annaple	
	Alfonso			Manda			Anwyl	
	Alonsa			Mandi			Arabel	
	Alonso			Mandie			Arabella	
	Alphondo			Mandy			Arrabella	
	Alphonsine		amb	Ambrese			Hannabell	
	Alphonso			Ambros			Mab	
	Lonnie			**Ambrose**			Mabel	
alr	**Alaric**			Ambrosina			Mabell	
alt	Aleta			Ambrosse			Mabella	
	Aletha			Ambrus			Mabelle	
	Alethea			Embrose			Mable	
	Alithea			Emrys			Maybel	
	Althea		amd	**Almond**			Maybelle	
alu	Alpheaus		ame	Almeina			Meave	
	Alpheus			**Almena**		amn	**Aminta**	aml
	Alphoeus			Almina			Araminta	mey
alv	Alvar			Elmena			Arraminta	
	Alvarah			Elmina		amo	Amo	amu
alw	Ailwyn	aln	amh	**Amariah**			**Amos**	
	Alden			Amaris			Amose	
	Aldwin		ami	Amchia			Amoss	
	Aldwyn			Amica			Amus	
	Alvan			**Amice**		amr	**Amaryllis**	
	Alven		aml	Aimee	amn	amu	Amor	amo
	Alvena			Aimie	emm		**Amorous**	
	Alverna			Am	eli	ana	Anastasia	eus

58

code	name			code	name			code	name	
	Anastatia				Dreena				Hanam	
	Anstes				Drena				Hane	
	Anstey				Drina				Hanh	
	Anstice			**ane**	Aneira	ned			Hann	
	Anstis				Aneirin				Hanna	
	Anstiss				**Aneurin**				Hannagh	
	Stacey				Nye				Hannah	
	Stacie				Nyrene				Hanne	
	Stacy			**ang**	Angel				Hannh	
	Statia				**Angela**				Hannie	
anc	Anchor	ask			Angelica				Nan	
	Anchoret				Angelina				Nance	
	Anchoretta				Angelo				Nancey	
	Ancrait				Angie				Nancy	
	Ancras				Angle				Nanette	
	Ancret				Angy				Naney	
	Ancreta			**ann**	Aannah	agn			Nanie	
	Angharad				Aina	bee			Nanis	
	Ingaret				Aine	chr			Nann	
and	And	ale			Ainthe	hos			Nanney	
	Andera	rhe			An	joa			Nannie	
	Anderina				Ana	nin			Nanny	
	Anders				Anae	sus			Nans	
	Anderson				Anah				Nany	
	Anderston				Ane				Nina	
	Andr				Anetta				Nita	
	Andra				Anika			**ano**	**Anslow**	
	Andraw				Anita			**ans**	Ancel	era
	Andraye				**Ann**				Ancelm	lan
	Andrea				Anna				Ancilla	wil
	Andreana				Annae				Ansell	
	Andreas				Annah				**Anselm**	
	Andrette				Anne				Anselma	
	Andreu				Anneka				Aselma	
	Andrew				Annetta				Selma	
	Andrewe				Annette				Zelma	
	Andrewina				Anney			**ant**	Anth	joa
	Andria				Annie				Anthea	tat
	Andrienne				Annika				Anthi	
	Andrietta				Annita				Anthoinus	
	Andrina				Anny				Anthoney	
	Andro				Anya				Anthonie	
	Androe				Eithne				Anthonies	
	Androu				Ena				Anthonij	
	Androw				Ethne				**Anthony**	
	Androwe				Exannah				Anthonye	
	Andw				Han				Anthoy	
	Andy				Hana				Antione	
	Anndra				Hanah				Antjuan	
	Dandy				Hanaha				Antoinette	

	Anton			Gilleasbuig			Ashlee	
	Antone		**are**	**Artemas**			Ashleigh	
	Antoney			Artemisia			**Ashley**	
	Antoni		**arg**	Argate			Ashlie	
	Antonia			**Argent**			Ashwell	
	Antonie		**ari**	**Ariadne**			Astley	
	Antonius			Ariane		**ask**	Anchetil	anc
	Antony		**arl**	**Arley**			Anchitel	
	Antuan		**arn**	Arnaud			Anketil	
	Antwan			Arnie			Anketin	
	Arbuthnot			**Arnold**			Ansketil	
	Tony			Arnoldine			Anskettell	
anu	Aeneas	aug		Arnot			**Asketil**	
	Angus			Arnott		**aso**	**Ashton**	
	Angusina		**art**	Art	eat		Aston	
	Aonghas			Artair		**asp**	**Aspasia**	
	Enas			Arter			Spash	
	Eneas			Arterei		**asr**	**Asher**	
	Ennis			Arthene		**ast**	Asta	
anw	**Anwen**			Arther			**Astrid**	
	Anwyn			Arthour			Estrid	
aph	Afra			**Arthur**		**ata**	**Atalanta**	
	Aphra			Arthure		**ate**	**Athene**	
	Epaphroditus			Arthuretta		**ath**	**Athelstan**	
apl	**Alpin**			Arthuri		**atk**	**Atkinson**	
	Alpine			Arthurina		**atl**	**Athalia**	
app	Abbelina			Artie			Athelia	
	Applina			Artina		**atn**	**Athanasius**	
	Appoline			Artis			Athanye	
	Appollo			Artisidilla		**ato**	**Athol**	
	Appolonia			Arty		**aub**	Albery	
aqu	**Aquila**			Aruther			Auberon	
ara	Areta			Ather			**Aubrey**	
	Aretas			Athur			Aubry	
	Aretha			Aurther			Elvera	
arc	Arch			Aurthur			Elvira	
	Archabald			Auther			Oberon	
	Archbald			Author		**aug**	Agusta	anu
	Archbd			Authur			Agustine	chr
	Archbold			Earthur			Agustus	hug
	Archd		**aru**	**Araunah**			Anagusta	
	Archer			Horanah			Augstin	
	Archibald		**asa**	**Asa**			August	
	Archiball		**ase**	**Asenath**			Augusta	
	Archibold			Asketh			Augustas	
	Archie			Azenath			Auguste	
	Archy			Sena			Augustin	
	Baldie		**ash**	Ash			Augustine	
	Eairdsidh			Ashey			Augustins	
	Gilleasbaig			Ashlea			Augustinus	

Codes giving Variants

Code	Name	
	Augustus	
	Austen	
	Austin	
	Austine	
	Austis	
	Auston	
	Austyn	
	Gus	
	Gussie	
	Gustas	
	Gustav	
	Gustave	
	Gustavus	
	Osston	
	Ostan	
	Osten	
	Ostin	
	Oston	
aur	Arelia	
	Aurea	
	Aurelia	
	Aurelian	
	Aureole	
	Auriel	
	Oralia	
	Oriel	
ave	April	
	Avaril	
	Averhilda	
	Averil	
	Averilda	
	Everalda	
	Everhilda	
	Everild	
avi	Ava	eve
	Aveas	
	Aves	
	Avice	
	Avis	
	Avisa	
avl	Alvedine	
	Alverdine	
aza	**Azariah**	
	Zaria	
azl	**Azalea**	
	Zelie	
	Zelina	
azu	**Azubah**	
	Zuba	
baa	**Balthasar**	

Code	Name	
bab	**Bal**	
	Bala	
bad	**Baldric**	
	Baudrey	
bae	**Beau**	
	Beaumont	
bag	**Bagshaw**	
bah	**Bathsheba**	
	Bathshua	
	Bersaba	
	Bethsheba	
	Sheba	
bai	**Bailey**	
bak	**Banks**	
bal	**Baldwin**	
	Maldwyn	
bam	**Barrymore**	
ban	Barnabas	ber
	Barnabus	
	Barnaby	
	Barne	
	Barney	
	Barny	
bao	**Bardolph**	
bap	**Baptist**	
	Baptista	
bar	Bab	boi
	Babbie	eli
	Babs	
	Barabal	
	Barbar	
	Barbara	
	Barbarah	
	Barbaraye	
	Barbarie	
	Barbaro	
	Barbarra	
	Barbary	
	Barber	
	Barbera	
	Barbery	
	Barberye	
	Barbie	
	Barbra	
	Barby	
	Baubie	
bas	**Basil**	
	Basilia	
	Basilla	
	Bassil	

Code	Name	
	Bazil	
	Vasilis	
bat	**Bart**	
	Barthol	
	Bartholemew	
	Bartholmew	
	Bartholmewe	
	Bartholomew	
	Bartholomewe	
	Barthw	
	Bartle	
	Bartlet	
	Bat	
	Bathurst	
	Batson	
	Batty	
	Bertholemi	
	Portholan	
	Tolly	
bau	**Baruch**	
bay	Barrie	bia
	Barry	
baz	Barzilla	
	Barzillai	
bda	**Baden**	
bde	**Bead**	
bea	**Beat**	
	Beata	
	Beaton	
	Beatria	
	Beatrice	
	Beatrices	
	Beatrix	
	Beatty	
	Bee	
	Betrice	
	Betriche	
	Betrix	
	Betteras	
	Betterice	
	Bettrice	
	Bettrys	
	Tris	
	Trissie	
	Trix	
	Trixie	
bed	**Bede**	
bee	**Benedict**	ann
	Benedicta	ben
	Benita	

code	name	var	code	name	var	code	name	var
	Bennet			Benny		bls	Blaise	
	Bennett			Berihert			**Blase**	
bef	**Bedford**			Bingamin		blu	**Bluebell**	
beg	Berengaria			Biniamen		bly	**Blith**	
	Berenger		beo	**Benoni**			Blithman	
beh	**Berthold**		ber	Barnard	ban		Blyth	
bei	Berenice	ber,bih		Barnet	bei		**Blythe**	
	Bernice	eli		Barnett	nad		Blythman	
	Berry	lyn		Bernadette		bma	**Bamber**	
	Bunny	ver		Bernadine		bna	**Baron**	
bek	Barclay			**Bernard**			Barron	
	Berkeley			Bernet		bne	**Benson**	
bel	**Belinda**	lyn		Bernhard		bno	**Bonar**	
bem	Bartram	alb		Bernie		bnr	Barnel	
	Bertram			Burnard			**Bernal**	
	Bertrand		bes	**Bevis**		bnt	**Bentley**	
ben	Banjamin	bee	bet	Berta	alb	boa	**Bonaventure**	
	Banjan	reu		**Bertha**	eli	boc	**Boadicea**	
	Bemjamin			Berther	rob	bod	**Brodie**	
	Ben			Berthia		boe	**Boyce**	
	Benejaman			Birtha		boi	Bonabel	eli
	Bengaman			Talbertha			**Bonita**	bar
	Bengamin		beu	**Beula**			Bonnie	joa
	Bengeman			Beulah			Bonny	
	Bengn		bev	Bev		bol	**Bolton**	
	Beniamin			**Beverley**		bon	**Bonamy**	
	Beniamini		bew	**Berwyn**		boo	**Booth**	
	Benj		bey	**Beryl**		bor	**Boris**	
	Benja			Burrill		bos	**Boswell**	
	Benjaby		bia	**Barrington**	bay	bow	**Bowman**	
	Benjam		bic	**Birch**		boy	**Boy**	
	Benjaman		bih	**Berenthia**	bei	boz	**Boaz**	
	Benjamen		bil	**Brinley**		bra	Brad	
	Benjamie		bin	**Binns**			**Bradley**	
	Benjamin		bir	**Birdie**		brc	**Brice**	
	Benjamine		bka	**Baker**			Bryce	
	Benjamn		bkr	**Barker**		brd	Bedelia	del
	Benjamon		bla	Bianca			Biddie	
	Benje			**Blanch**			Biddy	
	Benjeman			Blanche			Bidy	
	Benjiaman			Blanchiam			Bregit	
	Benjiman			Blauncha			Bride	
	Benjimin			Blinnie			Bridger	
	Benjm		blc	**Blackburn**			**Bridget**	
	Benjman		bli	**Blaine**			Bridgett	
	Benjmin		blk	**Blake**			Bridgget	
	Benjmn		blm	**Blossom**			Bridgit	
	Benjn		blo	**Blodwen**			Bridgitt	
	Benn			Blodwyn			Brigdet	
	Bennie		blr	**Blair**			Briget	

	Brigett		**bth**	Bethan	eli		Cammy	
	Brigid			**Bethany**		**can**	Candace	cao
	Brigit			Bethune			Candes	
	Brigitta		**btn**	**Brent**			Candia	
	Britt		**bto**	**Barton**			Candice	
	Gita		**btr**	**Brett**			**Candida**	
bre	Blenda		**bud**	**Bud**			Candy	
	Branden			Buddy		**cao**	Caddie	can
	Brandon		**bul**	**Butler**			Cadelia	car
	Breedon		**bun**	**Bruno**			Calorine	cel
	Brenainn		**bur**	**Burnet**			Caraline	cha
	Brenda			Burnitt			Caralyn	cor
	Brendan		**but**	**Bunty**			Cariline	mad
	Brenden		**bve**	**Bevan**			Carlene	
brf	**Beresford**			Bevin			Carlin	
	Berresford		**bwr**	**Brewster**			Carline	
brg	**Brigham**		**bya**	**Bayne**			Carloine	
brh	**Bradshaw**		**byd**	**Bryden**			Carlyn	
bri	Brain		**byo**	**Boyd**			Caro	
	Brian		**byr**	**Byron**			Carol	
	Briana		**caa**	**Caesar**			Carola	
	Brianus			Caezer			Carole	
	Briony			Ceaser			Carolin	
	Brya			Cesar			Carolina	
	Bryan			Seasar			**Caroline**	
	Bryon			Sezar			Carolyn	
brk	Brock		**cab**	**Campbell**			Carr	
	Brook		**cad**	Cadwalladar			Carraline	
	Brooke			**Cadwalleder**			Carrie	
	Brooksbank			Cardwalader			Carrilion	
brl	**Brilliana**		**cae**	**Carmel**			Carrol	
brm	**Bramwell**			Carmen			Caroline	
	Branwell			Charmaine			Carry	
brn	**Brunhild**	hid		Charmian			Cary	
bro	Branwen			Sharmain			Caryl	
	Bronwen			Sharmaine			Charoline	
brr	**Broderick**			Sharman			Karleen	
brs	**Barnes**			Sharmane			Karol	
brt	Britania		**cah**	Chapel			Lina	
	Britannia			**Chappell**		**cap**	**Captain**	
	Britney		**cal**	Calab		**car**	**Cara**	cao
	Brittan			**Caleb**			Caradoc	cha
	Brittany			Caleby			Caradog	kat
bru	**Bruce**			Caleh			Carina	shr
brw	**Brown**			Call			Carita	
bry	**Bryn**			Calob			Carrisa	
	Brynly		**cam**	Cam	mil		Carys	
	Brynmor			Camelia			Cerdic	
bsa	**Bassett**			**Camilla**			Ceredig	
bte	**Barrett**			Cammie			Charis	

	Charitie			Cissy		Arlette	cao
	Charity			Ecelia		Cahrles	car
	Cherie			Secilia		Carey	cor
	Cherry			Seelia		Carl	shr
	Kara			Selia		Carla	ter
	Sherry			Sheila		Carley	
cas	Casandra	ale		Shelagh		Carlie	
	Casey	kat		Shelah		Carlo	
	Cass			Shelia		Carlos	
	Cassandra			Sicil		Carlotta	
	Cassey			Sicila		Carly	
	Cassia			Sicilia		Chales	
	Cassie			Sicily		Challotte	
	Cassius			Sile		Chalotte	
	Cassy			Sis		Chalrotte	
	Caster			Sisley		Char	
cat	**Calvert**			Sissie		Chares	
cbo	**Corben**			Sissy		Charl	
	Corbin			Syssely		Charlene	
cda	**Cadell**			Sysselye		**Charles**	
cec	Caecile	jul	ced	**Cedric**		Charlesworth	
	Cecelia	shi		Cedrych		Charlet	
	Cecil	sil	ceh	**Chester**		Charlett	
	Cecila			Chet		Charlette	
	Cecile		cei	**Ceinwen**		Charley	
	Ceciley		cel	Celena	cao	Charlie	
	Cecilia			**Celeste**		Charline	
	Cecilie			Celestine		Charlis	
	Cecill			Celina		Charllote	
	Cecily			Salena		Charllotta	
	Ceclia			Salina		Charllotte	
	Celia			Sele		Charloote	
	Ceselia			Selena		Charlot	
	Cicel			Selestria		Charlote	
	Ciceley			Selin		Charlotee	
	Cicelia			Selina		Charlott	
	Cicelie			Selinah		Charlotta	
	Cicely			Selinda		Charlotte	
	Cicial			Seline		Charlottee	
	Cicil			Silena		Charls	
	Cicile			Silina		Charolette	
	Cicilia			Solina		Chars	
	Cicilie			Zelinda		Chas	
	Cicill		cep	**Cephas**		Chatty	
	Cicily		cer	**Ceridwen**		Chay	
	Ciliscia		ces	**Cresswell**	cre	Chere	
	Ciselia		cey	Ceris		Cheryl	
	Cislea			Cerris		Chick	
	Cisley			**Cerys**		Chls	
	Ciss		cha	Arletta	air	Chrles	

Codes giving Variants

	Chs		Christana		Cristan
	Chuck		Christane		Cristane
	Karl		Christann		Cristian
	Lotitia		Christanna		Cristiana
	Lottie		Christean		Cristiane
	Lotty		Christeane		Cristin
	Scharlotte		Christen		Cristina
	Sharleen		Christena		Cristofer
	Sharlet		Christephir		Criston
	Sharlot		Christian		Cristopher
	Sharlott		Christiana		Cristover
	Sharlotte		Christianah		Crustian
	Sharyl		Christiane		Crustina
	Sheralyn		Christianna		Crystal
	Sherilyn		Christibella		Extop
	Sherralyn		Christie		Extopher
	Sherralynn		Christien		Ina
	Sheryl		Christin		Ino
	Siari		Christina		Kerstie
	Tearlach		Christine		Kersty
	Tottie		Christinia		Kester
	Totty		Christn		Kidd
chd	**Chad**		Christo		Kirstan
che	**Chloe**		Christofer		Kirstane
	Cloe		Christoferus		Kirsten
chh	**Chedham**		Christoffer		Kirsty
	Cheetham		Christon		Kit
chl	**Chelsea**		Christoper		Kris
chm	**Champion**		Christoph		Kristina
chn	**Chandra**		Christophe		Kristoffer
cho	**Charlton**		**Christopher**		Tina
chp	**Chapman**		Christopheri		Xopher
chr	Cairistiona	ann	Christopherus		Xphofer
	Chirstian	aug	Christophr		Xpo
	Chirsty	cle	Christor		Xpofer
	Chisthopher	kat	Christouer		Xpoferi
	Chr		Christr		Xpoferus
	Chrestane		Christy		Xpoffer
	Chris		Christyan		Xpofferi
	Chrisandra		Christyfer		Xpofferus
	Chrisr		Chrus		Xtian
	Chrissie		Chursty		Xto
	Chrisstopher		Ciorstaidh		Xtopher
	Christ		Cirstane		Xtopheri
	Christabel		Cirstin	chs	**Christmas**
	Christabell		Cirsty	cht	**Chantal**
	Christabella		Crissey	chu	**Chauncy**
	Christain		Crissie	chy	**Chrysogon**
	Christaine		Crissy		Grisigion
	Christan		Cristaine	cla	**Claira**

Code	Name	Variant
	Claire	
	Clara	
	Clarabelle	
	Clarah	
	Clarance	
	Clare	
	Clarence	
	Clari	
	Claribel	
	Clarice	
	Claricy	
	Clarinda	
	Clarindo	
	Clarissa	
	Clarissia	
	Clarrie	
	Clarry	
	Cleris	
	Clorinda	
clc	**Clancy**	
cld	**Claud**	
	Claude	
	Claudeen	
	Claudelle	
	Claudette	
	Claudia	
	Claudina	
	Claudine	
	Claughton	
	Gladis	
	Gladness	
	Gladuse	
	Gladwys	
	Gladys	
	Gwladys	
cle	Cleem	chr
	Clem	
	Clemence	
	Clemency	
	Clemens	
	Clement	
	Clementia	
	Clementina	
	Clementine	
	Clemina	
	Clemmey	
	Clemmie	
cli	Cliff	
	Clifford	
	Clifton	

Code	Name	Variant
clk	**Clark**	
	Clarke	
	Clerk	
clm	Cole	coy
	Coleman	nic
	Coley	
	Colm	
	Colman	
cln	Clint	
	Clinton	
clo	**Clodagh**	
clp	Clea	
	Cleo	
	Cleopatra	
	Cleophas	
clr	Clarimente	
	Clarimond	
clt	**Clotilda**	
clu	Calam	ken
	Callum	mal
	Calum	
	Colum	
	Columba	
	Columbina	
	Columbine	
	Cullam	
clv	**Clive**	
cly	Clay	
	Clayton	
cma	**Cameron**	
cno	**Colonel**	
cnr	**Conroy**	
cnw	**Cornwallis**	
coa	**Conrad**	cos,cou
cob	**Corbett**	
cod	**Carden**	del
	Cordelia	
	Cordie	
coe	Corneilus	cos
	Cornelia	hel
	Cornelias	
	Cornelious	
	Cornelius	
	Cornellius	
	Corneluis	
	Cornenilius	
	Cornes	
	Cornie	
	Curnialus	
cog	**Coleridge**	

Code	Name	Variant
coi	**Collingwood**	
cok	**Cook**	
col	**Conal**	con
	Connell	
com	**Comfort**	
	Comforta	
con	**Conan**	col
	Connant	
coo	**Cosmo**	
cop	**Cooper**	
	Cowper	
cor	Cora	cao
	Corabelle	cha
	Coral	dor
	Corale	kee
	Coralie	lyn
	Coraline	
	Coranea	
	Coretta	
	Corina	
	Corinna	
	Corinne	
	Coroline	
	Correen	
	Corry	
	Kora	
	Korrein	
cos	Con	coa
	Conn	coe
	Connie	con
	Connor	cow
	Constance	
	Constancy	
	Constanie	
	Constant	
	Constanten	
	Constantia	
	Constantina	
	Constantine	
	Constartia	
	Constophia	
	Consuelo	
	Costin	
cot	**Colston**	
cou	**Courtenay**	coa
	Courtney	cur
	Curt	
	Kurt	
cov	**Colville**	
cow	**Conway**	cos

Codes giving Variants

coy	Colley	clm		Hyacinthe			Danice	
	Collis			Jacinta			**Daniel**	
cra	**Craig**			Jacinth			Daniele	
crb	**Crosby**			Jacintha			Daniell	
cre	**Cressida**	ces		Saint			Daniella	
	Cressy			Sanchia			Danielle	
crf	**Crofton**			Science			Danielus	
crg	**Creighton**			Sence			Danil	
	Crighton		cyp	Ciprian			Danile	
crh	**Crowther**			**Cyprian**			Danill	
cri	Chrispin			Zyprian			Danise	
	Crispian		cyr	**Cyril**			Danita	
	Crispin			Cyrilla			Danl	
	Crispiny		cyu	**Cyrus**	rus		Danll	
crl	**Corleana**		daa	**Damaris**	tam		Dann	
crm	**Crompton**			Dameris			Danna	
crn	Carleton			Damris			Danne	
	Carlton			Demas			Danneall	
cro	**Corisande**			Mara			Danniel	
crr	**Carter**			Marah			Danniell	
crs	**Carson**			Maraquitta			Danny	
crt	**Critchlow**			Tamaris			Dansea	
crv	**Craven**		dac	**Dacian**			Dansey	
crw	**Crawford**		dae	Daran	dra		Dansy	
csa	**Castle**			Daren			Danuel	
csi	**Casimir**			Daron			Danya	
cta	**Cater**			**Darren**			Danyele	
cur	**Curtis**	cou		Daryn			Danyell	
cut	Cathbert	alb	dag	**Dagmar**			Danzie	
	Cudbart		dah	**Dahlia**			Danzy	
	Cudberde			Dalia			Deiniol	
	Cudbert		dal	Dal			Deinol	
	Cuddie			**Dale**			Domhnall	
	Cuddy		dam	Daemon		dap	Daff	
	Cutbard			Dalmen			Daffie	
	Cutberd			Damen			**Daphne**	
	Cutbert			**Damian**			Daphny	
	Cuth			Damon		dar	Darcey	
	Cuthbert		dan	Daiel	don		**Darcy**	
	Cuthbertus			Dan		das	**Dallas**	
	Cuthbt			Dana		dat	**Dalton**	
	Cuthbte			Danal		dav	Daffyd	lav
	Cutherbert			Dane			Dai	
	Cuthr			Daneal			Daibhidh	
cvo	**Colvin**			Daneen			Daived	
cyi	**Cyriack**			Danel			Dathi	
	Syriack			Danella			Dav	
cyn	Cimmie	luc		Danette			Davd	
	Cynthia			Dani			Dave	
	Hyacinth			Danial			Davet	

	Davey		deh	**Denham**			Dermod
	David		dei	Dadie			**Dermot**
	Davide			Dede			Diarmuid
	Davidi			Deidra			Kermit
	Davidina			**Deidre**		dep	Delphi	phi
	Davie			Deidrie			**Delphine**
	Davied			Deirdre			Philadelphia
	Davin			Dierdrie			Philidelphia
	Davina		del	Del	ada		Phillidelphia
	Davinia			**Delia**	brd	der	**Derek**	edw
	Davis			Deliah	cod		Derenda	ric
	Davit			Delila	dle		Deric
	Davy			Delilah	eli		Derreck
	Daw			Della			Derrick
	Dawson		dem	Des			Derrie
	Day			**Desmond**			Derry
	Deio		den	Den	tey		Deryck
	Devany			Denes			Dirk
	Devina			Denice		des	Desiderata
	Dewey			Denies			**Desire**
	Dewi			**Denis**			Desiree
	Divina			Denise			Dysory
	Dvd			Deniss		det	**Delta**
	Taffy			Denness		dev	**Denver**
	Veda			Dennet		dex	**Dexter**
	Vida			Denney		dez	**Denzil**
daw	**Dawn**			Dennis		dia	**Diamond**
day	Darell			Dennison		dig	**Digby**
	Darleen			Denny		dil	Dille	dyl
	Darlene			Dennys			**Dilys**
	Darley			Denys			Dyllis
	Darrell			Dinas			Dylus
	Darryl			Dinis		din	Deana
	Daryl			Dinnis			Deanna
dco	**Doctor**			Diogenes			Deanne
dea	**Delmar**			Diones			Deena
deb	Daborah			Dionis			Dena
	Deb			Dionisius			Di
	Debbie			Dionne			Diana
	Debora			Dionys			Dianah
	Deborah			Dionysia			Diane
	Deborough			Dionysius			Dianiah
	Deborrah			Diot			Dianna
	Debra			Dynas			Diannah
	Debrah			Dyonis			Dianne
	Devorah			Dyonisius			Dina
	Devra			Dysnysius			**Dinah**
dec	Decima			Dyson			Dinnah
	Decimus		deo	Darby	jer	dio	**Diggory**
ded	**Desdemona**			Derby		div	**Divarus**

Codes giving Variants

	Divers			Doll	eud		Dothy	
	Diverus			Dolley	hel		Dotty	
	Dives			Dolly	isi		Dthy	
dla	Daley			Dora	lau		Orah	
	Daly			Dorah		dot	**Donnet**	
dle	Delice	del		Dorate		dou	Dong	
	Delicia			Dorath			Doug	
	Delise			Doratha			Dougal	
dne	**Dean**			Dorathea			Dougald	
dnt	Dent			Dorathee			Dougall	
	Denton			Dorathie			**Douglas**	
doc	Dorca			Dorathy			Douglass	
	Dorcas			Doratie			Doyle	
	Dorcase			Doreley			Dug	
	Dorcus			Dorete			Dugal	
	Dorkis			Doretha			Dugald	
doe	Doirean	dor		Dorethe			Dugd	
	Doreen			Dorethy			Dughall	
	Dorena			Dorice			Dughlas	
	Dorene			Doris		dow	**Downs**	
	Doria			Doritha		dra	Dar	dae
	Dorian			Dorithe			**Dara**	
	Dorinda			Dorithie			Darah	
	Dorrien			Dorithy			Daratie	
dol	Delores	dor		Dorithye			Daria	
	Dolores			Doritie			Darias	
	Lola			Dority			Darie	
	Lolita			Doritye			Darius	
dom	**Dominic**	nic		Doroothy		drm	**Drummond**	
	Dominica			Doroth			Drumond	
	Dominick			Dorotha		dro	Drew	
	Dominy			Dorothe			**Drogo**	
	Domnick			Dorothea		dru	Drewsila	
	Donna			Dorotheam			Drucella	
don	Doileag	dan		Dorothee			Drucilla	
	Don			Dorothey			Druscilla	
	Donal			Dorothia			Drusila	
	Donald			Dorothiae			**Drusilla**	
	Dond			Dorothie			Drusylla	
	Donella			**Dorothy**		dud	**Dudley**	
	Donkin			Dorotiae		due	**Duene**	
	Donnella			Dorrathy		dul	Dawsabell	
	Donnie			Dorretey			Delsie	
doo	Donavon			Dorrit			Dousabell	
	Donovan			Dorrothy			Dow	
dor	Diorbhail	ado		Dorthea			Dowe	
	Dodie	cor		Dorthy			Dowsabel	
	Dodo	doe		Dorythe			Dowse	
	Dolena	dol		Dorytye			Dowsland	
	Dolina	edw		Dot			Dulce	

69

	Dulcibel		edn	**Edna**	edw			Edwood	
	Dulcibella			Ednah				Edword	
	Dulcie		edr	**Edred**				Edwrd	
	Dulsebe		edt	Edan	ada			Edwyne	
	Dulsebella			Ede	edg			Eideard	
	Dulsie			Eden				Emund	
dun	Donnchadh			Edena				Eward	
	Dun			Edeth				Fedora	
	Duncan			Edie				Feodora	
dur	Dante			Edina				Iola	
	Durand			**Edith**				Iolo	
	Durante			Editha				Iorwerth	
dus	**Dunstan**			Edyth				Ned	
dwa	Duane			Eyde				Neddy	
	Dwain			Yden				Odwin	
	Dwaine		edw	Eadie	der			Ted	
	Dwayne			Eame	dor			Teddy	
dwi	**Dwight**			Eamon	edn			Tewdwr	
dye	**Dyer**			Ed	jul			Thea	
dyl	Dillian	dil		Edd	ter			Theadosia	
	Dillon			Eddie	the			Theo	
	Dylan			Eddy	thh			Theodocia	
dym	**Dymphna**			Edm	thp			Theodora	
	Dympna			Edman				Theodore	
dyo	**Dymoke**			Edmand				Theodoric	
ead	**Eardley**			Edmd				Theodorus	
ean	**Earnshaw**			Edmee				Theodosia	
ear	**Earl**			Edmnd				Todius	
	Earlene			Edmond				Tudor	
	Erle			Edmonde				Yorath	
eat	**Earth**	art		Edmont				Yoruth	
	Eartha			Edmund		egb	**Egbert**		
ebe	Benezer			Edmunde		ege	**Egerton**		
	Ebbaneza			Edmundi		egl	Eglantine		
	Eben			Edmundus			**Eglentyne**		
	Ebeneer			Eduardi		eil	**Eilwen**		
	Ebenesar			Eduardus			Eilwyn		
	Ebeneser			Edvardi		eir	**Eira**		
	Ebenezar			Edvardus		eki	**Ekin**		
	Ebenezer			Edvy		ela	**Elam**		
	Ebenezr			Edw		elb	**Elba**		
	Ebenzer			**Edward**		eld	Elden		
edb	**Edborough**			Edwarde			Eldine		
	Edborowe			Edwardi			Elding		
edg	Adair	edw		Edwards			**Eldon**		
	Edgar			Edwardus		ele	Elaza	ali
	Ogier			Edwd			Eleasar	eli
edi	**Edric**			Edwin			**Eleazar**		
	Edrice			Edwina			Eleazer		
	Edrus			Edwn			Eliezer		

Codes giving Variants

	Elizar		Bettsy		Elizab
	Elizea		Betty		Elizabath
	Elizer		Bety		Elizabeath
	Elizia		Bithia		Elizabeht
	Lazarus		Bithiah		Elizabella
	Leneazer		Bitty		Elizabet
elg	**Elgiva**		By		**Elizabeth**
eli	Ailsa	ada	Bythia		Elizabetha
	Ailspit	ali	Ealasaid		Elizabethae
	Babette	aml	Eelizabeth		Elizabetham
	Batheanna	bar	Eilish		Elizabethe
	Bathia	bel	Eiz		Elizabett
	Bathya	bet	Eiza		Elizabh
	Beathag	boi	Eizabeth		Elizabith
	Beathea	bth	Eizabth		Elizabth
	Bell	del	Elazabeth		Elizaebth
	Bella	ele	Elce		Elizaeth
	Bellah	lel	Elesabeth		Elizah
	Belle	mil	Elesbeth		Elizath
	Besey	sop	Elesebeth		Elizb
	Bess		Elesha		Elizbeath
	Besse		Elespet		Elizbeth
	Bessey		Elezabath		Elizbt
	Bessie		Elezabeth		Elizbth
	Bessy		Elezabethe		Elizeabath
	Bet		Elezabth		Elizebath
	Beta		Elezbeth		Elizebeth
	Betey		Elezebeth		Elizebethae
	Beth		Eliab		Elizebth
	Betha		Eliabeth		Elizh
	Bethea		Elie		Elizsabeth
	Betheah		Elisa ·		Elizt
	Bethel		Elisab		Elizte
	Bethenia		Elisabeh		Elizth
	Bethia		Elisaberth		Ellceana
	Bethiah		Elisabeth		Ellesebeth
	Bethie		Elisabetha		Ellisabeth
	Betina		Elisabethae		Elliza
	Betsay		Elisaeth		Ellizabeth
	Betsee		Elisah		Elsa
	Betsey		Elisbeth		Elsabeth
	Betsie		Elisebeth		Elsabethe
	Betsy		Elish		Elsbeth
	Bett		Elispeth		Elsen
	Bette		Elissa		Elseth
	Betteria		Elissabeth		Elsie
	Bettey		Elisth		Elsiemeana
	Bettie		Elixabeth		Elsp
	Bettina		Eliz		Elspa
	Bettsey		Eliza		Elspat

Code	Name	Variant
	Elspath	
	Elspet	
	Elspeth	
	Elspie	
	Elspit	
	Elspith	
	Elspitt	
	Elspot	
	Elspt	
	Elspth	
	Elysabeth	
	Elysabethe	
	Elyzabeth	
	Elyzabetha	
	Elyzabethe	
	Elz	
	Elza	
	Elzab	
	Elzabath	
	Elzabeth	
	Elzbth	
	Elzth	
	Esabell	
	Esabella	
	Esabelle	
	Esibell	
	Ezabella	
	Ezit	
	Iassabel	
	Ib	
	Ibbie	
	Ilse	
	Isa	
	Isab	
	Isaballa	
	Isabel	
	Isabela	
	Isabell	
	Isabella	
	Isabellah	
	Isabelle	
	Isabla	
	Isable	
	Isabol	
	Isbald	
	Isbel	
	Isbell	
	Isbella	
	Iseabail	
	Isebella	

Code	Name	Variant
	Ishbel	
	Isibel	
	Isible	
	Isla	
	Isobel	
	Isobell	
	Isobella	
	Isoble	
	Issa	
	Issabel	
	Issabell	
	Issabella	
	Issabelle	
	Issobel	
	Issobell	
	Issobella	
	Issoble	
	Izabel	
	Izabell	
	Izabella	
	Izable	
	Izaell	
	Libbie	
	Libby	
	Libella	
	Lieser	
	Lisa	
	Lisbeth	
	Lise	
	Lisette	
	Lissie	
	Liza	
	Lizbeth	
	Lizey	
	Lizy	
	Lizzee	
	Lizzie	
	Lizzy	
	Tetsy	
	Tetty	
	Tib	
	Tibby	
	Tibia	
	Tissy	
	Titty	
	Tity	
	Veta	
	Yesbell	
elj	Elejea	ali
	Eli	

Code	Name	Variant
	Elias	
	Eligah	
	Eligha	
	Elihu	
	Elija	
	Elijah	
	Eliot	
	Elisha	
	Elliot	
	Elliott	
	Ellis	
	Ely	
elk	Elcaney	
	Elkanah	
ell	**Ellery**	
elm	Aylmer	
	Elmer	
elt	**Elton**	
elu	Elluned	lyn
	Eluned	
	Luna	
	Luned	
elv	Ailbhe	
	Alby	
	Alvy	
	Elva	
	Elvis	
ema	Emanual	emm
	Emanuel	hym
	Emmanuel	
	Emmanuelle	
	Emuel	
	Immanuel	
	Manny	
	Manuel	
eme	Emaretta	emm
	Emer	
	Emeria	
	Emerita	
	Emeritta	
	Emerson	
	Emery	
	Emmerson	
emm	Amalia	aml
	Amelia	ema
	Amelinda	eme
	Ameline	erm
	Amellia	lyn
	Amilia	
	Amley	

Ammy			Emmelina			**Ermintrude**	get
Em			**Emmeline**	ern	Earnest	
Ema			Emmely		Erna	
Emala			Emmer		**Ernest**	
Emaline			Emmet		Ernestine	
Emaly			Emmie		Ernie	
Emblem			Emmila		Ernst	
Emblen			Emmily	ers	Arskein	
Embler			Emmot		Arskine	
Emblin			Emmott		Eresken	
Eme			Emmy		Erskin	
Emelena			Emn		**Erskine**	
Emeley			Emne	ery	**Eryl**	
Emeli			Emota	esa	Emerald	ism
Emelia			Emott		**Esmeralda**	
Emeline			Emotte		Meraud	
Emely			Emy	ese	**Esebeloue**	
Emelyn			Emye	eso	**Esmond**	
Emey			Emylyn	ess	**Essex**	
Emiah			Erma	est	Eacy	hen
Emil			Ima		Easter	ter
Emila			Imally		Easther	
Emile			Imblen		Ehster	
Emilen			Irma		Eshter	
Emiley			Melena		Ess	
Emilia			Melia		Essie	
Emilie			Melias		Esta	
Emiliene			Melina		Estelle	
Emiline	end	**Enderby**		Ester	
Emilly	eng	**English**		Estha	
Emily	eni	**Enid**		**Esther**	
Emla	eno	**Enoch**		Hadassah	
Emlen		Enock		Hessie	
Emley		Enos		Hessy	
Emlia	eph	Eph	eup	Hester	
Emlin		Ephm		Hesther	
Emly		Ephraim		Stella	
Emlyn		Ephrain		Stilla	
Emm		Ephram	esu	Esan	
Emma		Ephrame		**Esau**	
Emmah		**Ephriam**		Esaw	
Emmala	era	Elmo	ans	Esiau	
Emmalah		**Erasmus**	eta	**Ethan**	
Emmaline		Erismoth	ete	**Etherton**	
Emmaly	eri	**Erin**	eth	Audie	alb
Emmar		Eryn		Audrey	
Emmat		Hibernia		Awdrie	
Emme		Iverna		Dee	
Emmeat		Juverna		Ethe	
Emmeby	erm	Armigil	emm	Ethel	

	Ethelbert			Euphem			Eziekel	
	Ethelburg			Eupheme			Zeke	
	Etheldred			**Euphemia**		ezr	Ez	
	Etheldreda			Euphemie			**Ezra**	
	Ethelia			Euphen		faa	**Faramond**	
	Ethelinda			Euphens		fab	Fabia	
	Ethelred			Euphimia			**Fabian**	
	Ethelwyn			Euphin		fae	**Farewell**	
	Ethra			Euphmia		fai	Faiethe	
	Ethylinda			Euphrem			**Faith**	
	Theldred			Oighrig			Faithful	
eti	**Etain**			Phemie			Fay	
	Etaoin			Uphemia			Faye	
eub	**Eubule**		eus	**Eustace**	ana		Fayth	
euc	**Euclid**			Eustacia			Faythe	
eud	**Eudora**	dor	evd	**Evadne**			Fidel	
eue	**Eusebius**		eve	Aveline	avi		Fidelia	
eug	Eoghan	joh		Avenel	hel		Fidelis	
	Eugene	vir		Eva		fal	Fairlay	
	Eugenia			Evaline			**Farley**	
	Eugenie			Evangeline		fam	**Farmer**	
	Eugine			Eve		fan	**Farnham**	
	Gena			Eveleen		far	**Farquhar**	
	Gene			Evelina			Fearchar	
	Ginny			Eveline		faw	**Fawcett**	
eul	**Eulalia**			**Evelyn**		fea	Feather	
	Lallie			Evie			**Featherstone**	
eun	Enice			Evita		fee	**Fereshteh**	
	Eunice			Hevah		feg	Fearghus	
	Unice		evr	**Everard**			Feargus	
	Unis			Everet			Fergie	
eup	Effie	eph		Everitt			**Fergus**	
	Effim	fra		Ewart			Ferguson	
	Effum	hep	ewe	Eoghann	joh		Fhearghais	
	Effy			Euan		fel	Fernleigh	
	Eithrig			Euen			**Fernley**	
	Epham			Ewan		fen	Fenella	pen
	Ephie			**Ewen**			Finola	
	Ephy			Ewin			Fiona	
	Eppie			Owain			Fionnghal	
	Epsy			Owen			Nella	
	Eufeme			Owena			Nuala	
	Euph			Owin		fer	Fardy	
	Euphaim			Ywain			Ferdenand	
	Eupham		eze	Ezakea	ish		Ferdenando	
	Euphame			Ezakiah	zac		**Ferdinand**	
	Euphan			Ezeikel			Ferdinanda	
	Euphane			Ezekiah			Ferdinando	
	Euphans			Ezekial			Ferrand	
	Euphean			**Ezekiel**			Ferry	

Code	Name		Code	Name		Name	Code
fes	**Festus**			Forster		Fransciscus	
fet	**Fenton**		**fon**	**Fountain**		Franses	
few	**Fenwick**		**for**	Fortunatus		Fransis	
fie	Field			**Fortune**		Franz	
	Fielding		**fos**	**Foster**		Fras	
fif	**Fife**		**fou**	**Foulds**		Fraunc	
fih	**Firth**		**fow**	**Fowler**		Fraunce	
fin	Findlay		**fra**	Fancy	eup	Fraunces	
	Findley			Fane		Frauncis	
	Finlay			Faney		Fraunciscus	
	Finley			Fann		Frcis	
	Fionnlagh			Fanna		Myfanwy	
	Frang			Fanney		Phanah	
fir	Firman			Fannie		**fre**	Eric	alf
	Firmin			Fanny		Erica	fit
fis	**Fisher**			Fany		Erika	win
fit	**Fitz**	fre		Fenna		Federick	wlf
	Fitzarthur			Fenne		Fred	
	Fitzgerald			Ffrancis		Freda	
	Fitzjohn			Fiance		Fredc	
	Fitzroy			Fraces		Freddy	
	Fitzwalter			Fran		Frederic	
	Fritz			Franc		Frederica	
	Fritzroy			**Frances**		Frederich	
fla	Flavia			Francesca		**Frederick**	
	Flaviana			Francescus		Fredericus	
	Flavilla			Francess		Fredica	
	Flavius			Francie		Fredick	
fle	**Fletcher**			Francies		Fredirick	
flo	Finghin			Francine		Fredk	
	Fleur			Francis		Fredr	
	Flo			Francisc		Fredrck	
	Flora			Francisca		Fredreck	
	Floraidh			Franciscae		Fredric	
	Florance			Francisci		Fredrica	
	Florella			Francisco		Fredrich	
	Florence			Franciscus		Fredrick	
	Florentina			Francises		Fredrik	
	Florina			Franciska		Fredrk	
	Floris			Franciss		Freeda	
	Florrie			Franck		Freida	
	Flory			Francoise		Frieda	
	Flossie			Francs		Rica	
	Flower			Francus		Rickie	
	Floy			Francys		Rika	
	Flurry			Frank		**fri**	**Friday**
fob	**Forbes**			Frankie		Frideswide	
foe	Forest			Franklin		Frideswyde	
	Forester			Franncis		Friswith	
	Forrest			Frans		Frizwith	

	Frysewede	
	Fryswyth	
frm	Free	
	Freedham	
	Freedom	
	Freeman	
frn	**Friend**	
frr	**Farrell**	
frs	Fraise	
	Fraser	
	Frazer	
	Friese	
fue	**Fuller**	
ful	Fawke	
	Foulk	
	Fowke	
	Fulk	
fyt	Fitch	
	Fytch	
gab	Gabe	
	Gabel	
	Gabi	
	Gabriel	
	Gabriell	
	Gabriella	
	Gabrielle	
	Gabrilla	
	Gaby	
gac	**Garrick**	ger
gad	**Garland**	
gae	**Garfield**	
gaf	**Galfrid**	
gai	Caio	kat
	Caius	
	Caw	
	Gaius	
	Gias	
gal	**Galahad**	
gam	Gam	jam
	Gamaliel	
	Gamaliell	
	Gamel	
	Gamma	
	Gem	
	Gemelle	
	Gemma	
	Gemmel	
gan	**Garner**	
gao	**Gaylord**	
gar	**Gareth**	ger

	Garth	
gas	Gascagne	
	Gascoigne	
	Gascoygne	
	Gascoyne	
	Gaston	
gav	Garven	
	Gavan	
	Gaven	
	Gavin	
	Gavyn	
	Gawain	
	Gawen	
	Gawin	
	Gawn	
gay	**Gay**	
	Gaye	
gea	**Gresham**	
ged	**Gerda**	
gee	**Green**	
	Greene	
	Greenwood	
	Grenne	
gef	Geffraye	
	Geffrey	
	Geoff	
	Geoffery	
	Geoffray	
	Geoffrey	
	Geoffry	
	Geofrey	
	Geve	
	Giff	
	Godfery	
	Godfray	
	Godfrey	
	Godfrus	
	Godfry	
	Godiva	
	Jefery	
	Jeff	
	Jefferey	
	Jefferies	
	Jefferson	
	Jeffery	
	Jeffray	
	Jeffree	
	Jeffrey	
	Jeffrie	
	Jeffry	

	Jeoffrey	
geh	**Gethro**	
gei	**Geraint**	
gen	**Gent**	
	Genty	
geo	Dod	
	Geo	
	Geoarge	
	Geoe	
	Geog	
	Geogana	
	Geoganna	
	Geoge	
	Geogre	
	Geor	
	Geordie	
	Georg	
	Georgana	
	Georganna	
	George	
	Georgeana	
	Georgeanna	
	Georgeina	
	Georgena	
	Georges	
	Georgette	
	Georgia	
	Georgiana	
	Georgianna	
	Georgie	
	Georgiena	
	Georgii	
	Georgij	
	Georgina	
	Georgine	
	Georginia	
	Georginna	
	Georgium	
	Georgius	
	Georguis	
	Geroge	
	Goerge	
	Goergeanna	
	Gorg	
	Gorge	
	Seoras	
ger	Garald	gac
	Gare	gar
	Garrat	jer
	Garret	

76

	Garrett				Egidius		glo	**Gloria**		
	Garrie				Gelda			Glorianna		
	Garry				**Gilda**			Glorie		
	Gary				Gilder			Gloris		
	Gerald			gid	**Gideon**			Glory		
	Geraldine			gie	Geiles		gly	Glennis	gue	
	Geralt				Geillis			Glenys	gwe	
	Gerard				Geills			Glinys		
	Geri				Geils			**Glyn**		
	Gerrald				Gileas			Glyndor		
	Gerrard				**Giles**			Glyndwr		
	Gerrold				Gilius			Glynis		
	Gerry				Gilles		gma	Garmon		
	Jerald				Gillies			Germaine		
	Jeraldine				Gilo			**German**		
	Jerold				Gilse			Jarman		
	Jerrold				Gyles			Jerman		
ges	Gersham				Gyllon			Jermyn		
	Gershom				Jiles		goa	**Goodman**		
	Gershon			gif	**Gifford**	alb		god	**Goddard**		
	Gerson			gil	Gib	jul		Godderd		
get	Gartrite	erm			Gibbie		goe	Golden		
	Gartrude				Gibbon			Goldie		
	Gatesen				Gibbun			Golding		
	Gateson				Gibby			**Goldwin**		
	Gatty				Gibe		gol	**Goliath**		
	Gert				Gibeon			Golliath		
	Gertie				Gibson		gom	**Gomer**		
	Gertrude				Gibun		gon	**Goronwy**		
	Gerty				**Gilbert**		gor	Gordan		
	Girtrude				Gilberta			Gorden		
	Trud				Gilbertus			Gordie		
	Truda				Gilbride			**Gordon**		
	Trudi				Gylbert		gow	Godith		
	Trudie			gin	**Grainne**			Godly		
	Trudy				Grainnia			Godlyne		
gev	Garvis				Grania			Godric		
	Gerius			gip	**Gipsy**			**Godwin**		
	Geruase			gir	Gildero			Goodeth		
	Geruis				Gilderoy		gra	**Grace**		
	Gervas				Gildray			Gracey		
	Gervase				Gildri			Gracia		
	Gervis				Gildroy			Gracie		
	Gervise				**Gilroy**			Gracilia		
	Jarvis			gis	Ghislaine			Gratia		
	Jervas				Gisela			Gratiae		
	Jervase				**Gisele**		gre	Greer		
	Jervice			git	**Githa**			Greg		
	Jervis			gla	**Gladstone**			Gregery		
gia	Egidia			gln	**Glanville**			Gregg		

	Gregor		
	Gregorij		
	Gregory		
	Grigor		
grh	Graeme		
	Graham		
	Grahame		
gri	Griff		
	Griffes		
	Griffin		
	Griffith		
	Gruffold		
	Gruffydd		
grl	**Greville**		
grm	**Grimbald**		
grn	**Grant**		
gro	**Grover**		
	Groves		
grs	Girsal		
	Girsall		
	Girsel		
	Girzel		
	Girzil		
	Griesel		
	Grisal		
	Grisel		
	Griselda		
	Grisell		
	Grisiel		
	Grisiell		
	Grissal		
	Grissall		
	Grissel		
	Grissell		
	Grissil		
	Grissill		
	Grizal		
	Grizall		
	Grizel		
	Grizell		
	Grizzel		
	Grizzle		
	Selda		
	Zelda		
grt	**Grantley**		
grv	**Granville**		
	Grenville		
grw	**Grimshaw**		
gry	**Gray**		
	Grey		

gte	Geth	
	Gethen	
	Gethin	
gue	Gaenor	gly
	Gainerr	joa
	Gains	joh
	Gayna	vir
	Gaynah	wan
	Gayner	
	Gaynor	
	Geneva	
	Genevieve	
	Genevra	
	Ginette	
	Ginevra	
	Ginnette	
	Guenevere	
	Guenor	
	Guinevere	
	Gwenhwyfar	
	Jenefer	
	Jenifer	
	Jennie	
	Jennifer	
	Jenny	
	Vanora	
	Wander	
	Wannore	
	Wannour	
gui	**Guiscard**	
gul	**Guildford**	
	Guilford	
gun	**Gunilda**	
	Gunnell	
	Quenild	
gur	**Gurney**	
guy	Guido	
	Guy	
	Guyat	
	Guyryve	
	Wyat	
gwe	Glen	gly
	Glenda	win
	Glenn	
	Glenna	
	Guendolen	
	Gwen	
	Gwenda	
	Gwendolen	
	Gwendoline	

	Gwendolyn	
	Gwendy	
	Gweneth	
	Gwenillian	
	Gwenllean	
	Gwenllian	
	Gwenn	
	Gwenneth	
	Gwennie	
	Gwenyth	
	Gwyn	
	Gwyneth	
	Gwynne	
haa	**Hallam**	
hac	**Halcyon**	
had	**Handel**	
hae	Hand	
	Handley	
	Hanley	
haf	**Halford**	
hag	**Hagar**	
	Haggar	
hah	**Hawthorn**	
	Hawthorne	
hai	**Haidee**	
hak	**Havelock**	
hal	**Haldane**	
ham	Ham	
	Hamby	
	Hamet	
	Hamlet	
	Hamlin	
	Hamlyn	
	Hammet	
	Hammond	
	Hamnet	
	Hamo	
	Hamon	
	Hamond	
han	Hannibal	
	Hannibel	
hao	**Hamilton**	
hap	**Happy**	
har	Enrico	hay
	Enry	hen
	Errol	
	Hailey	
	Hal	
	Haley	
	Hall	

78

Codes giving Variants

Halley			Hnry		Eileen	joa
Hank			Hny		Eilidh	lau
Hanry			Hry		Eilleen	leo
Haralda			Parry		Eily	mad
Haray			Penry		El	nei
Harold	has		Hargrave		Elaine	oli
Haroldene			**Hargreaves**		Elaner	
Harray	hat		**Hartley**		Elanor	
Harrey	hau		**Harcourt**		Elayne	
Harrie	hav		Harvet		Ele	
Harris			**Harvey**		Elean	
Harrison			Hervey		Eleanah	
Harrold	haw		**Harwood**		Eleaner	
Harry	hax		**Haxby**		Eleanor	
Harrye	hay		**Hayley**	har	Eleanora	
Hary	haz		Haselwood		Eleener	
Heenery			Hazael		Elein	
Hen			Hazal		Elen	
Henary			**Hazel**		Elena	
Henderson			Hazeline		Elener	
Hendre			Hazell		Eleni	
Hendrie			Hazelle		Elenner	
Hendrik	hbe		**Hebden**		Elenor	
Hendry			Hebdon		Elenora	
Henerey	hea		Heath		Elenr	
Henerici			**Heather**		Eleoner	
Henericus	heb		**Hebe**		Eleonor	
Henery			Heber		Eleonora	
Henerye			Hebor		Eleonore	
Henie	hec		Eachann		Elianor	
Hennerie			Eachdoin		Elianora	
Hennery			**Hector**		Elin	
Henney			Hectorina		Elina	
Hennry	hed		Headley		Elinar	
Henor			**Hedley**		Eliner	
Henr			Hedly		Elinn	
Henrey	hee		**Hereward**		Elinnor	
Henri	heg		Elga		Elinor	
Henrici			Elgra		Elinore	
Henricus			**Helga**		Elinour	
Henrie			Olga		Elioner	
Henrik	hei		Hallewell		Elionor	
Henry			Hellewell		Ella	
Henrye			**Helliwell**		Ellalina	
Henryk	hel		Aibhlin	ada	Ellan	
Henury			Aileen	agn	Ellanor	
Heny			Annora	ala	Elleanor	
Herald			Ealoner	coe	Ellen	
Heryc			Eeanor	dor	Ellena	
Hindrie			Eibhlin	eve	Ellenar	

Ellener	Helina		Arminda
Ellenner	Heline		Arminel
Ellennor	Helison		Harman
Elleno	Hell		**Herman**
Ellenor	Hellan		Hermia
Elley	Hellein		Hermoine
Elleypane	Hellen		Hermon
Ellia	Hellena	**hen** Etta	est
Elliane	Hellenae	Etty	har
Ellianor	Hellence	Hariet	hew
Ellidth	Hellin	Hariett	
Ellie	Hellon	Hariot	
Ellimah	Helyn	Hariott	
Ellin	Hlen	Harrat	
Elline	Honer	Harreit	
Elling	Honner	Harreitt	
Ellinn	Honnor	Harret	
Ellinor	Honnour	Harrett	
Ellinr	Honor	Harriat	
Ellionora	Honora	Harriatt	
Ellon	Honorah	Harriet	
Ellona	Honore	Harriete	
Ellunor	Honoria	Harriett	
Ellyn	Honour	Harrietta	
Ellynor	Hyla	Harriette	
Elner	Ilean	Harriot	
Elnor	Ileen	Harriott	
Elnye	Ilene	Harrit	
Elon	Lana	Harritt	
Elonar	Lane	Harrot	
Eloner	Leanora	Harrott	
Elonor	Lena	Harrt	
Elot	Lenora	Harruet	
Elyn	Lenore	Hart	
Halina	Leonara	Harty	
Hallen	Leonora	Haryat	
Hannar	Nell	Hattie	
Hanner	Nelley	Hatty	
Hanorah	Nellie	Heneretta	
Helah	Nellon	Henerietta	
Helean	Nelly	Henerita	
Helein	Nonie	Heneritta	
Helen	Nora	Heniretta	
Helena	Norah	Henny	
Helenam	Noreen	Henreitta	
Helene	Oner	Henretta	
Helener	**hem** Armand	Henriatta	
Helenn	Armando	Henrieta	
Helenor	Armin	**Henrietta**	
Helin	Armina	Henriette	

80

Code	Name	Var	Code	Name	Var	Code	Name	Var
	Henritta		hir	**Hiram**	hym		Hywel	
	Heriot			Hirom		hra	**Harper**	
	Herriet			Huram		hrd	Harden	
	Herriett			Hy			Hardisty	
	Herriot			Hyam			**Hardy**	
	Hette			Hyrum			Hardyman	
	Hettie		hit	**Hilton**		hre	**Hero**	
	Hetty			Hylton		hrl	**Harley**	
	Netty		hne	Henaghan		hro	**Harrop**	
	Yetta			**Heneage**		hrr	**Harrington**	
heo	**Herod**		hoa	**Howard**		hsa	**Hastings**	
hep	**Hephizibah**	eup	hob	**Hornby**		hua	**Haugh**	
	Hephsibah			Hornsby		hug	Aodh	aug
	Hephzabah		hod	**Holden**			Heugh	
	Hephzebah		hoe	Horne			Hew	
	Hephzebay			**Horner**			Hewet	
	Hephzibah		hof	Horsell			Hewgh	
	Hepsey			**Horsfall**			Hewghe	
	Hepsibah		hol	**Holland**			Hewin	
	Hepsie			Holley			Hewitt	
	Hepsy			Hollie			How	
	Hepzabah			Hollis			Huey	
	Hepzibah			Holly			**Hugh**	
	Hepzibeth		hom	Holman			Hughe	
her	Archelaus			Holmes			Hughes	
	Hercula			**Homer**			Hughey	
	Hercules		hon	Hon			Hughie	
hes	**Hesketh**			**Honey**			Hughina	
het	**Heaton**		hop	**Hope**			Hugo	
hew	Hedda	hen		Hopeful			Hugoi	
	Hedwig			Hopestill			Hugois	
	Hedy		hor	Hod			Hugonis	
	Hetta			Horace			Huisdean	
hey	**Henley**			Horatia			Hutchinson	
hez	Hez			**Horatio**			Huw	
	Hezekiah			Horatius			Uisdean	
hia	**Haines**			Horrace		hul	**Hulda**	
hid	**Hilda**	brn		Horry			Huldah	
	Hilde			Hurrish		hum	Dump	ola
	Hildebrand			Orris			Dumphry	
	Hildegard			Orry			Homfrey	
	Hildred		hos	**Hosanna**	ann		Humfrey	
	Hylda			Hosannah			Humfridus	
hil	**Hilary**			Hosen			Humfry	
	Hill			Hoson			Humph	
	Hillary			Osanna			Humphery	
	Hillery		hot	**Hortensia**			**Humphrey**	
	Hilorie		how	Hoel			Humphry	
hip	**Hippolyta**			Howel			Humphrye	
	Hippolyte			**Howell**			Hwmffrey	

	Hwmfrey		ire	Eireen	may			Isador	
	Omfray			Eirene				Isadora	
	Umfray			Irena				**Isidore**	
hun	**Hunter**			**Irene**		ism	Emony	aml
	Huntly			Reenie			Esme	esa
hya	**Hayward**			Rena			Esmee	
hym	Chaim	ema		Renate			Ishmael	
	Hayyim	hir		Rene			**Ismay**	
	Hyman			Renee			Ismena	
	Hymen			Renie			Ismenia	
	Hymie			Rennie			Jesmond	
hyp	**Hypatia**		iri	**Iris**		iso	**Isolda**	
ian	**Ianthe**		irv	Ervin			Isolde	
ica	**Icarus**			Erwin			Isolte	
ich	**Ichabod**			Irvin			Isot	
ida	**Ida**			Irvine			Isott	
	Idabell			**Irving**			Izot	
ido	Edony			Irwin			Yseult	
	Idonia			Urwin			Ysolda	
idr	**Idris**		isa	Esakiah	zac		Ysonde	
idw	**Idwal**			Ike		isr	Isarel	isi
ign	Ignacious			Ikey			Iseral	
	Ignas			**Isaac**			**Israel**	
	Ignatia			Isaacc			Israell	
	Ignatious			Isaack			Isreal	
	Ignatius			Isaacs			Issy	
	Inigo			Isaak			Izzy	
	Jenico			Isac		ith	**Ithel**	
ili	**Illingworth**			Isacc		iva	Iva	joh
ill	**Illtyd**			Isach			**Ivah**	
ima	**Imalda**			Isack		ivo	Ives	ivr
	Imelda			Isacke			Ivette	
imo	**Imogen**			Isaic			**Ivo**	
	Imogene			Isake			Ivon	
	Imogine			Iseac			Yvette	
ina	Igor			Issac			Yvon	
	Inga			Issacar			Yvonne	
	Inge			Issachar		ivr	Ifor	ivo
	Ingeborg			Izaak			Iomhair	
ine	**Innes**			Izaat			Iomhar	
	Innis		ish	Ezia			Iver	
ing	Ingmar			Hezia			Iveson	
	Ingraham			Heziah			Ivie	
	Ingram			Isaah			**Ivor**	
	Ingrid			Isah			Ivoreen	
inh	**Ingham**			**Isaiah**			Ivorine	
inn	**Innocent**			Isaih			Ivy	
ion	**Iona**			Isiah			Yvor	
	Irona		isi	Dore	dor	jab	Jabas	
ira	**Ira**			Dory	isr		Jabaz	

Code	Name	Variant 1	Variant 2
	Jabe		
	Jaber		
	Jabes		
	Jabesh		
	Jabey		
	Jabez		
	Jabus		
	Jebez		
jac	Jacaline	jam	
	Jacalyn	joh	
	Jackie		
	Jacky		
	Jaclyn		
	Jacolyn		
	Jacqualynn		
	Jacqueline		
	Jacquelyn		
	Jacquetta		
	Jacqui		
	Jaquelina		
	Jaqueline		
jad	**Jade**		
jae	**Jael**		
	Jaell		
jak	**Jackson**		
jam	Hamish	gam	
	Iago	jac	
	Ja	jca	
	Jacques	jes	
	Jaes		
	Jago		
	Jaime		
	Jam		
	Jamar		
	Jame		
	James		
	Jamesin		
	Jamesina		
	Jamesing		
	Jameson		
	Jamesyng		
	Jamie		
	Jamieson		
	Jamima		
	Jamis		
	Jammey		
	Jammima		
	Jams		
	Jamsie		
	Janes		

Code	Name	Variant 1	Variant 2
	Jas		
	Jay		
	Jayme		
	Jeames		
	Jem		
	Jemima		
	Jemimah		
	Jemina		
	Jemma		
	Jemmima		
	Jemmina		
	Jemmy		
	Jim		
	Jimima		
	Jimmima		
	Jimminer		
	Jimmy		
	Jirmirna		
	Jm		
	Mima		
	Seamus		
	Seumas		
	Seumus		
	Shamus		
	Sheumais		
jan	Jasmin	joa	
	Jasmine		
	Jessamine		
	Yasmin		
	Yasmina		
	Yasmine		
jap	Casper	kat	
	Jasper		
	Jesper		
jar	**Jared**		
	Jaro		
jas	**Jason**		
	Jayson		
jav	**Javan**		
	Javin		
	Javon		
jca	Jacabus	jam	
	Jackobenna	joa	
	Jacob		
	Jacoba		
	Jacobi		
	Jacobina		
	Jacobine		
	Jacobj		
	Jacobus		

Code	Name	Variant 1	Variant 2
	Jake		
jco	**Jocasta**		
jed	Ged		
	Jed		
	Jeddia		
	Jedidiah		
jeh	**Jehu**		
	Jehudijah		
jep	Japheth		
	Jephtha		
	Jephthah		
	Jephunneth		
	Jeptha		
jer	Gerome	deo	
	Jarius	ger	
	Jeramye		
	Jereh		
	Jeremh		
	Jeremia		
	Jeremiah		
	Jeremie		
	Jeremy		
	Jerimiah		
	Jermiah		
	Jerome		
	Jerry		
jes	Jasse	jam	
	Jese	joa	
	Jesea		
	Jesie		
	Jess		
	Jessa		
	Jesse		
	Jessee		
	Jesses		
	Jessey		
	Jessica		
	Jessie		
	Jessy		
	Jusica		
	Seasaidh		
jet	**Jethro**		
	Jeturah		
jew	Jeuis	joe	
	Jewes		
	Jewess		
jez	Jezabell		
	Jezebel		
	Jezebell		
jho	**Joah**		

joa	Chavon	agn		Jenit			Johannes
	Jaen	ann		Jenitt			Johanney
	Jain	ant		Jenna			Johannie
	Jaine	boi		Jennat			Johannis
	Jaines	gue		Jennet			Johanus
	Jana	hel		Jennett			Johas
	Janae	jan		Jennetta			Johnanna
	Janam	jca		Jenney			Jonat
	Janat	jes		Jennit			Jone
	Jane	joh		Jennitt			Jones
	Janell	jos		Jhoanna			Jonet
	Janene	nal		Jhohan			Jonett
	Janessa	vir		Jinney			Jonnet
	Janet			Jinny			Jonnett
	Janeta			Jnet			Juanita
	Janett			**Joan**			Loanna
	Janetta			Joana			Seonag
	Janette			Joanah			Seonaid
	Janey			Joane			Shavon
	Janice			Joanes			Sheena
	Janie			Joanet			Shena
	Janis			Joanis			Sheona
	Janit			Joann			Shevon
	Jann			Joanna			Shiven
	Jannat			Joannae			Sian
	Janne			Joannah			Sina
	Jannet			Joanne			Sine
	Jannett			Joannes			Sinead
	Jannetta			Joannis			Siobahn
	Jannette			Joas			Sioban
	Jannot			Joene			Siobhan
	Jannott			Johaes			Wanita
	Janot			Johais			Zane
	Jant			Johames		job	Joab
	Jayne			Johan			**Job**
	Jean			Johana			Jobe
	Jeane			Johanah			Jobey
	Jeanette			Johane			Jobie
	Jeanie			Johanem			Joby
	Jeanit			Johanes		joc	Achim
	Jeanne			Johaneta			**Joachim**
	Jeannie			Johani			Jochem
	Jeannit			Johanis		joe	Jewel	jew
	Jenat			Johanj			Jewell
	Jenet			Johann			**Joel**
	Jeneta			Johanna		jof	**Joffre**
	Jenete			Johannah		joh	Ean	eug
	Jenett			Johannas			Eion	ewe
	Jenette			Johanne			Eoin	gue
	Jeney			Johannem			Evan	iva

84

	Evans	jac		Jonathen			Jospeh	
	Hans	joa		Jonathn			Josph	
	Hanson			Jonathon			Jseph	
	Iain			Joneh			Sepp	
	Ian			Jonie		**jot**	**Jotham**	
	Ieuan			Jonn			Jothin	
	Iohn			Jonney		**jou**	Jesiah	jos
	Ivan			Jonny			Joseah	
	Ivana			Jonothan			Josh	
	Jack			Jonothon			Joshah	
	Jan			Jony			**Joshua**	
	Janner			Jonye			Joshuah	
	Jen			Sean			Joshue	
	Jenkin			Shaine			Josia	
	Jenkins			Shane			Josiah	
	Jevon			Shaun			Josias	
	Jhn			Shawn			Jossiah	
	Jho			Sion			Jossua	
	Jhon		**joq**	**Jonquil**			Josua	
	Jhone		**jor**	**Jordan**			Josuah	
	Jhonn			Judd			Josuha	
	Jn		**jos**	Hoseph	joa		Joziah	
	Jno			Jeseph	jou	**joy**	Jeoyse	
	Jock			Jo			Jocelin	
	Joh			Joe			Jocelyn	
	John			Joey			Joclyn	
	Johna			Johe			Joice	
	Johnathan			Johes			Joie	
	Johnathon			Johh			Josalene	
	Johne			Johis			Joscelin	
	Johnes			Johs			Joselene	
	Johnis			Joph			Josilene	
	Johnne			Jopseph			Joss	
	Johnny			Jos			Josse	
	Johns			Josa			Josslyn	
	Johnson			Jose			Joy	
	Johnsten			Joseh			**Joyce**	
	Johnston			Josep			Joycelyn	
	Johnstone			**Joseph**		**jub**	Jubal	
	Johnthan			Josepha			**Jubilee**	
	Jon			Josephe		**jud**	Juda	
	Jona			Josephene			**Judah**	
	Jonah			Josephi			Judas	
	Jonas			Josephine			Jude	
	Jonath			Josephn			Judia	
	Jonatha			Josephus			Yehudi	
	Jonathan			Joses		**jui**	Jodie	jul
	Jonathania			Josheph			Ju	
	Jonathanis			Josie			Judeth	
	Jonathas			Josp			**Judith**	

	Judithe	
	Judy	
jul	Gilian	cec
	Gill	gil
	Gillean	iol
	Gillet	jui
	Gillian	
	Gillianne	
	Gillie	
	Gillot	
	Gillson	
	Gillyanne	
	Gilson	
	Jellian	
	Jewett	
	Jill	
	Jillain	
	Jillet	
	Jillian	
	Jillianne	
	Jolyon	
	Jouls	
	Jowett	
	Judath	
	Juet	
	Juetta	
	Juilea	
	Jule	
	Jules	
	Juley	
	Julia	
	Juliah	
	Julian	
	Juliana	
	Juliann	
	Julianna	
	Julias	
	Julie	
	Julielmus	
	Julien	
	Juliet	
	Julius	
	Jullian	
	July	
	Julyan	
	Julyen	
	Leanne	
	Lianne	
jun	**June**	
jus	Iestin	

	Iestyn	
	Jestine	
	Justillian	
	Justin	
	Justina	
	Justine	
	Justinian	
	Yestin	
jut	**Justice**	
kan	Cain	
	Caine	
	Kane	
kat	Acacia	car
	Cacia	cas
	Cai	chr
	Caitlin	gai
	Carew	jap
	Cartharine	kee
	Catarina	
	Catarine	
	Cataryne	
	Cate	
	Caterane	
	Caterena	
	Caterina	
	Caterine	
	Catern	
	Cath	
	Catharam	
	Catharen	
	Catharin	
	Catharine	
	Cathe	
	Cather	
	Catheraine	
	Catheran	
	Cathereine	
	Catheren	
	Catherena	
	Catherin	
	Catherina	
	Catherine	
	Catherinr	
	Cathern	
	Catherne	
	Catheryne	
	Cathiriene	
	Cathirine	
	Cathleen	
	Cathn	

Cathne
Cathorine
Cathr
Cathrain
Cathraine
Cathrane
Cathrein
Cathren
Cathrin
Cathrine
Cathy
Catie
Catren
Catrin
Catrina
Catrine
Catriona
Catron
Ceit
Chatherine
Kass
Katarina
Kate
Kath
Kathar
Katharen
Katharin
Katharine
Katharyne
Kathe
Katheraine
Katheran
Katherein
Katheren
Katherene
Katherin
Katherina
Katherinam
Katherine
Kathern
Katherne
Katheryn
Katheryne
Kathleen
Kathlyn
Kathorne
Kathr
Kathren
Kathrene
Kathrin

86

Code	Name	Var
	Kathrinae	
	Kathrine	
	Kathron	
	Kathryn	
	Katie	
	Katina	
	Katran	
	Katren	
	Katrena	
	Katrina	
	Katrine	
	Kay	
	Keathran	
	Keathren	
	Kethrain	
	Kethrin	
	Ketty	
	Kittey	
	Kitty	
	Kity	
	Rina	
	Treena	
	Treina	
	Trena	
	Trina	
	Trinetta	
	Trinita	
kea	**Kendal**	
	Kendall	
keb	**Keble**	
ked	**Kennedy**	
kee	Car	cor
	Caren	kat
	Carin	kie
	Caron	
	Carren	
	Carrin	
	Carron	
	Caryn	
	Corah	
	Karen	
	Karena	
	Karina	
	Karrenappuch	
	Karrenhappuc	
	Kerah	
	Keren	
	Kerenhappuch	
	Keri	
	Keria	

Code	Name	Var
	Kerr	
	Kerri	
	Kerrie	
	Kerry	
kei	**Keith**	
kel	Calvin	
	Kalvin	
	Kelvin	
	Kelvyn	
ken	Coinneach	clu
	Kellem	
	Kem	
	Ken	
	Kena	
	Kendra	
	Kenelm	
	Keneme	
	Kenhelm	
	Kenia	
	Kenneth	
	Kennice	
	Kenny	
	Kenza	
	Kevan	
	Keverne	
	Kevin	
keo	**Kenton**	
ker	Kendrick	
	Kenerick	
	Kenrick	
	Kerrick	
kes	Kelcey	
	Kelsa	
	Kelsey	
	Kelsie	
ket	Kent	
	Kentigern	
keu	Kettura	
	Keturah	
	Kiturah	
kez	Kasia	
	Kazia	
	Kerziah	
	Kesia	
	Kesiah	
	Kessiah	
	Kethiah	
	Kezia	
	Keziah	
	Kissie	

Code	Name	Var
	Kizia	
	Kizzie	
kib	**Kirby**	
kie	Ciara	kee
	Keir	
	Keira	
	Keiran	
	Kiera	
	Kieran	
	Kyran	
kim	Kim	
	Kimberley	
	Kimberly	
	Kym	
kin	King	
	Kingsley	
	Kingston	
kir	**Kirk**	
kit	**Kirton**	
kni	**Knight**	
kyl	Kaylee	
	Kayley	
	Keala	
	Kealey	
	Kealy	
	Keeley	
	Keelie	
	Keeling	
	Keely	
	Keighley	
	Keiley	
	Keilly	
	Keily	
	Kelley	
	Kellie	
	Kelly	
	Kieley	
	Kieli	
	Kiley	
	Kyle	
	Kylee	
	Kylie	
lab	**Laban**	
lac	Lachlain	
	Lachlan	
	Lachland	
	Lachlanina	
	Lachlon	
	Lachunn	
	Lauchlan	

	Lauchlen			Lauretta			Livinia	
	Lauchlin			Laurice			Lovenah	
	Laughlan			Laurie			Loveviner	
	Laughlin			Lauriman			Lovina	
	Laughline			Laurina			Lovinia	
	Lochlan			Laurinda			Vina	
lad	Ladia			Laurine			Vincy	
	Lady			Law		law	**Lawton**	
lae	**Laverne**			Lawe		lay	**Layton**	
laf	**Layfield**			Lawranc			Leighton	
lag	**Langford**			Lawrance			Leyton	
lal	**Layland**			Lawrenc		lca	**Lacey**	
lam	Lambard			Lawrence			Lacy	
	Lambert			Lawrencii		lea	Leanda	
	Lambin			Lawrentii			**Leander**	
lan	Ancelot	ans		Lawrentius			Leandra	
	Enselin			Lawria		lee	Lester	les
	Lance			Lawrie		leh	Lea	
	Lancelin			Lawson			**Leah**	
	Lanceliott			Lolly			Lee	
	Lancelot			Lora			Lees	
	Lancelott			Lorances			Leigh	
	Lancelt			Loreen		lel	Laila	eli
	Lanceolett			Loren			Leila	
	Lannclot			Lorena			Lelah	
	Launce			Lorenzo			**Lelia**	
	Launceliot			Loretta			Lellie	
	Launcelot			Lori			Leyla	
lao	Lament			Lorin			Lil	
	Lamont			Lorinda			Lila	
lar	Lara			Loris			Lilas	
	Larisa			Lorrie			Lilia	
lau	Lanty	dor		Low			Liliah	
	Larace	hel		Lowe			Lilian	
	Larance	loa		Lowrance			Lilias	
	Larence	zeu		Lowrence			Lilius	
	Lari		lav	Labina	dav		Lilla	
	Larrence			Lavena	lev		Lillah	
	Larry			Lavenia	men		Lillas	
	Laura			Lavia	sil		Lilley	
	Lauranc			Lavina	vin		Lillian	
	Laurance			Laviner			Lillias	
	Laureance			**Lavinia**			Lilliaz	
	Laureen			Lavinie			Lillie	
	Laurel			Levena			Lilly	
	Lauren			Levener			Lily	
	Laurena			Levenia			Lyla	
	Laurence			Levina		lem	Lem	
	Laurentius			Levinia			Lemmy	
	Laurentus			Livina			**Lemuel**	

Code	Name	Var	Code	Name	Var	Code	Name	Var
len	**Lennox**		lew	Leuisa	aly	lit	**Linton**	
leo	Len	hel		Leusia	lod		Lynton	
	Lenard			Lew	loi	lle	Lewellen	lyn
	Lenda			Lewes	lov		Lewellin	
	Lenna			**Lewis**	luc		Llewelin	
	Lennard			Lewisa			Llewellin	
	Lenny			Lewys			Llewellyn	
	Lenoard			Lois			**Llewelyn**	
	Lenord			Lou			Llywelyn	
	Leo			Louella		llo	Floyd	
	Leon			Louesa			**Lloyd**	
	Leona			Louesia			Loyd	
	Leonard			Louezia		lly	Lear	
	Leonardus			Louie			**Llyr**	
	Leonie			Louis		loa	Loraine	lau
	Leopold			Louisa			Lorane	
	Lionel			Louise			Lorayne	
	Lona			Louisia			**Lorraine**	
	Lyon			Louiza			Lorrane	
	Lyonel			Lous			Lorrayne	
	Lyonell			Lousa		lob	**Lob**	
ler	**Leroy**			Louse		lod	**Lodowick**	lew
les	Les	lee		Lousea			Ludovic	
	Lesley			Lousia			Ludovick	
	Leslie			Lovis			Ludwig	
	Lesly			Lowis		lof	**Loftas**	
let	Laetitia			Lueiza			Lofthouse	
	Latitia			Luesa			Loftus	
	Leatitia			Luesea		lol	Love	
	Leta			Lueza			Lovel	
	Letesse			Luis			**Lovell**	
	Letice			Luisa			Lovet	
	Leticia			Lula			Lovett	
	Letita			Lulie			Lovey	
	Letitia			Lulu			Lovie	
	Letittia			Ouida		lom	**Lomas**	
	Lettesia		lic	**Lincoln**		lon	**Lonsdale**	
	Lettia		lid	**Lindsay**	lyn	lor	Lorn	
	Lettice			Lindsey			**Lorna**	
	Letticia			Lindzy			Lorne	
	Lettisia			Linsay		lot	**Lot**	
	Lettitia			Linsey		lov	**Loveday**	lew
	Lettuce			Linzi			Lovedy	lol
	Letty			Lyndsay			Lowday	
	Lititia			Lyndsey		low	**Lowry**	
	Tish			Lynsey		lro	**Lord**	
lev	**Levi**	lav		Lynsie		luc	Cindinia	cyn
	Levia		lil	**Lilith**			Cindy	lew
	Levins		lin	**Linus**			Leucy	
	Levy		lis	**Lister**			Lucas	

	Lucaser			Lyddia			Marsh	
	Lucasta			Lydea			Marsha	
	Luce			Lydeah		**mad**	Alena	ala
	Lucetta			**Lydia**			Alene	cao
	Lucette			Lydiah			Madaline	hel
	Lucey		**lyn**	Elinda	bel		Madalyn	
	Lucia			Linda	cor		Madelain	
	Lucian			Lindy	elu		Madelene	
	Lucie			Linnet	emm		Madelina	
	Lucien			Linney	lid		**Madeline**	
	Lucile			Lyn	lle		Maden	
	Lucilla			Lynda	lyo		Madilyn	
	Lucille			**Lynette**	mel		Madlen	
	Lucina			Lynn	pau		Madlin	
	Lucinda			Lynne	ros		Madline	
	Lucius			Lynnette	lyn		Madlyn	
	Luck		**lyo**	Linden			Mady	
	Luckie			Lindon			Magaden	
	Lucy			**Lyndon**			Magda	
	Lucye		**lyr**	**Lyra**			Magdalan	
	Luke		**lyu**	**Lyulf**			Magdalane	
	Lusia		**lyw**	Lynwen			Magdalen	
	Lusy			**Lynwyn**			Magdalena	
	Lusye		**maa**	Marena	mac		Magdalene	
	Sindy			**Marina**	may		Magdaline	
lum	**Lumley**			Marine			Magdallen	
	Lumly			Marna			Magdolon	
lup	**Lupton**			Marnie			Maidline	
lur	Lucrece			Merina			Maudlan	
	Lucrelia			Morina			Maudland	
	Lucretia		**mac**	Marc	maa		Maudlin	
	Lueretia			Marcell	mai		Maudlyn	
lut	**Luther**			Marcella	miz		Mawdeland	
lwe	**Lewin**			Marcellus		**mae**	Marla	may
lya	Lisle			Marcena			Marleen	
	Lyall			Marcene			Marlena	
lyd	Ledah			Marcha			**Marlene**	
	Ledea			Marci			Marlin	
	Lida			Marcia			Marlyn	
	Lidda			Marcie		**maf**	**Mansfield**	
	Lidday			Marcilyn		**mag**	Magnes	
	Liddayay			Marcina			**Magnus**	
	Liddia			Marcine			Manius	
	Liddiah			Marcius			Manus	
	Liddy			**Marcus**			Manyus	
	Lide			Marcy		**mah**	Malachi	
	Lidia			Mark			**Malachy**	
	Lidya			Marke			Malacky	
	Lyd			Markham		**mai**	Martaine	mac
	Lyda			Marsella			Martainn	mat

	Marten		Majorie	Margot
	Martin		Majory	Margraet
	Martina		Mar	Margrat
	Martine		Marg	Margrate
	Martinus		Margae	Margreat
	Marty		Margaet	Margreate
	Martyn		Margar	Margreatt
maj	**Major**		Margarat	Margreit
mal	Mal	clu	Margareet	Margret
	Malcolm		**Margaret**	Margreta
	Malcolme		Margareta	Margrete
	Malcom		Margaretae	Margrett
	Malkin		Margaretam	Margretta
mam	Dukana		Margarete	Margrette
	Duke		Margarett	Margrey
	Marduke		Margaretta	Margrit
	Marmaducem		Margarette	Margrot
	Marmaduke		Margarey	Margrt
man	**Manfred**		Margarie	Margry
mao	b		Margarit	Margt
	Madog		Margaritae	Marguarita
mar	Daisey	maa	Margarite	Marguerite
	Daisie	may	Margarrit	Marjary
	Daisy		Margart	Marjery
	Dasey		Margary	Marjorie
	Dasi		Margat	Marjory
	Dasie		Margatt	Marsail
	Greeta		Marge	Marsaili
	Greta		Marger	Masie
	Gretchen		Margerat	Massey
	Gretel		Margere	Massia
	Gretta		Margeret	Massie
	Madge		Margerett	Massy
	Mag		Margeria	Masy
	Magarct		Margerie	Maysie
	Mage		Margeritt	Mazey
	Mageria		Margerrit	Mazie
	Magertt		Margert	Meg
	Magery		Margery	Megan
	Magge		Margerye	Meggie
	Maggie		Marget	Mergeria
	Maggy		Margett	Mergrett
	Magot		Margha	Merjorie
	Magret		Margharita	Meta
	Magt		Margiad	Mgaret
	Maidie		Margie	Mgerye
	Mairead		Margit	Mgrett
	Maisie		Margo	Mgt
	Maisy		Margorie	Mgy
	Maizy		Margory	Mog

Code	Name	Var		Code	Name	Var		Name	Var
	Moggy				Mawrica			Mairwen	seo
	Mrgaret				Mawson			Mall	ver
	Mysie				Merrick			Malley	wil
	Pearl				Meuric			Mally	
	Peg				Meurig			Maly	
	Peggey				Meyrick			Mamie	
	Peggie				Morice			Manon	
	Peggotty				Morie			Marai	
	Peggy				Moris			Maralyn	
	Peigi				Morris			Maray	
	Perl				Morry			Maretta	
	Pog			mav	Mavies			Marey	
	Poggy				**Mavis**			Mari	
	Purly			maw	Math	mat		Maria	
	Reta				Matha			Mariabella	
	Rita				Mathaei			Mariae	
mas	**Manasseh**				Mathaeus			Mariah	
mat	Made	mai			Mathar			Mariam	
	Mat	maw			Mathei			Mariame	
	Mathilda	may			Mather			Marian	
	Matild	mrh			Mathes			Mariana	
	Matilda	pat			Matheus			Mariane	
	Matilday				Mathew			Mariann	
	Matildia				Mathewe			Marianna	
	Matt				Mathias			Marianne	
	Mattey				Matth			Marie	
	Mattie				Matthaei			Mariel	
	Mattilda				Mattheus			Marietta	
	Matty				**Matthew**			Mariette	
	Matw				Matthews			Marih	
	Maty				Matthias			Marilyn	
	Maud				Matthw			Marin	
	Maude				Mattw			Marinda	
	Maulde			max	Max			Marion	
	Mawd				Maxena			Marione	
	Mawde				Maxene			Marionica	
	Methilda				Maxime			Mariot	
	Metilda				**Maximilian**			Marioun	
	Mitilda				Maxina			Marious	
	Moade				Maxine			Maris	
	Petty				Maxwell			Marisa	
	Tilda			may	Madie	ire		Marita	
	Till				Mae	maa		Marius	
	Tillah				Maili	mae		Marllia	
	Tilley				Maille	mar		Marolyn	
	Tillie				Mair	mat		Maron	
	Tillot				Maira	mir		Marria	
	Tilly				Mairan	mur		Marriah	
mau	Marice	mos			Maire	pau		Marriam	
	Maurice				Mairi	rhe		Marriame	

Codes giving Variants

	Marrian	
	Marriana	
	Marriane	
	Marriann	
	Marrianna	
	Marriánne	
	Marrie	
	Marriea	
	Marrien	
	Marrin	
	Marrion	
	Marron	
	Marry	
	Mary	
	Marya	
	Maryan	
	Maryann	
	Maryanna	
	Maryanne	
	Marye	
	Maryjane	
	Marylyn	
	Maryon	
	Maura	
	Maureen	
	May	
	Maye	
	Mayrie	
	Mearye	
	Mella	
	Mennie	
	Meria	
	Meriah	
	Meriam	
	Meribah	
	Mhairi	
	Mhari	
	Mia	
	Miah	
	Mimi	
	Miria	
	Miriah	
	Miriam	
	Mirian	
	Mirran	
	Mirren	
	Mirriam	
	Mitzi	
	Moira	
	Moire	

	Moll	
	Mollie	
	Molly	
	Moreen	
	Moria	
	Moriah	
	Moureen	
	Moy	
	Moyra	
	Mureen	
	My	
	Myria	
	Myriam	
	Pallison	
	Pally	
	Polina	
	Polley	
	Polly	
	Pollyanna	
	Varey	
	Varie	
mcd	**Macdonald**	
	Mack	
	Mcdonald	
mea	**Merab**	
meb	**Melbourne**	
mec	Melcher	
	Melchior	
med	**Medora**	
mee	**Meredith**	mer
	Meridith	
	Merie	
	Merridith	
	Merry	
meh	**Mehetabel**	
mei	**Melville**	
mel	Malin	lyn
	Malina	
	Malinda	
	Melaine	
	Melanie	
	Melinda	
	Mellanie	
	Melloney	
	Mellony	
	Melonie	
	Melony	
mem	**Mendham**	
men	Malvina	lav
	Mel	

	Melva	
	Melvin	
	Melvina	
	Melvyn	
meo	**Melody**	
mer	Mearcy	mee
	Mearsey	
	Mercedes	
	Mercer	
	Mercey	
	Mercia	
	Mercier	
	Mercy	
	Mercye	
mes	**Meshach**	
met	**Methuselah**	
mev	Marvin	mur
	Marvyn	
	Merfin	
	Merlene	
	Merlin	
	Merlyn	
	Mervin	
	Mervyn	
mey	**Menty**	amn
	Minty	
mez	**Menzies**	
mha	**Mahala**	
	Mahalah	
	Mahalahah	
	Mahalar	
	Mahaler	
	Mahalia	
	Mahela	
	Mahelea	
	Mahlah	
	Malaha	
	Mehala	
	Mehalah	
	Mehalia	
mia	Milca	
	Milcah	
mib	Marabel	mir
	Marable	
	Marbella	
	Mirabel	
	Mirabella	
mic	Mechel	
	Mial	
	Mic	

	Micaell			Milson			Mazila
	Micah			Milton			Mesella
	Micahel			Myles			Messella
	Micaiah		mig	**Mignon**			Mezillah
	Mical			Mignonette			**Mizela**
	Michael		mii	**Meirion**			Mizelle
	Michaela			Merion			Myzel
	Michaelis			Merrion		mla	**Marlton**
	Michaell		mil	Melesina	cam	mli	**Melior**
	Michal			Meleta	eli		Meliora
	Michall			Melicent	mid		Mellear
	Micheal			Melissa			Melyear
	Micheall			Melita			Melyor
	Micheil			Melitta		mll	Millar
	Michel			Mellicent			**Miller**
	Michele			Mellie		mln	**Milner**
	Michell			Mellissa		mna	**Mansel**
	Michelle			Melusine			Mansell
	Michiel			Milicent		mnl	**Manley**
	Michl			Milison		mno	**Manoah**
	Mick			Mille		mod	**Monday**
	Mickell			Millecent		moe	**Modesty**
	Mickie			Millecente		mof	Morfudd
	Micky			Millesent			**Morfydd**
	Micl			Milleson		mog	Margain
	Miel			Milley			Morden
	Mighel			**Millicent**			**Morgan**
	Mihel			Millicenth		moi	**Moriarty**
	Mike			Millicentiae		mol	**Morley**
	Mitchel			Millie			Morly
	Mitchell			Millison		mom	**Mortimer**
	Myel			Milly		mon	Mona
	Myell			Missy			Monia
	Mygell		min	**Minerva**			**Monica**
	Myghell		mio	**Middleton**			Moyna
	Myller		mir	Maranda	ama	moo	Moor
mid	Meldred	mil		Mira	may		**Moore**
	Milborough			Mirah	mib	mor	**Mordecai**
	Milbrough			Miram	ran		Mordicai
	Milburh			Mirana		mos	Morton	mau
	Milbury			**Miranda**			Mose
	Mildred			Mirra			**Moses**
	Millbourn			Myra			Moss
mie	Mile			Myron			Mosses
	Milena		mit	**Maitland**			Moyes
	Miles		miy	Midgely			Moyse
	Milesa			**Midgley**			Mozes
	Mills		miz	Masella	mac	mot	**Montague**
	Milon			Mazala			Monty
	Milonis			Mazella			Mountague

Codes giving Variants

<table>
<tr><td>mov</td><td>Morven</td><td></td></tr>
<tr><td>mow</td><td>Morwenna</td><td></td></tr>
<tr><td>mra</td><td>Marshal</td><td></td></tr>
<tr><td></td><td>Marshall</td><td></td></tr>
<tr><td></td><td>Marshel</td><td></td></tr>
<tr><td>mre</td><td>Merle</td><td></td></tr>
<tr><td>mrh</td><td>Mart</td><td>mat</td></tr>
<tr><td></td><td>Marte</td><td></td></tr>
<tr><td></td><td>Marth</td><td></td></tr>
<tr><td></td><td>Martha</td><td></td></tr>
<tr><td></td><td>Marthar</td><td></td></tr>
<tr><td></td><td>Marthay</td><td></td></tr>
<tr><td></td><td>Marthe</td><td></td></tr>
<tr><td></td><td>Marther</td><td></td></tr>
<tr><td></td><td>Marthia</td><td></td></tr>
<tr><td></td><td>Martho</td><td></td></tr>
<tr><td></td><td>Marthy</td><td></td></tr>
<tr><td></td><td>Marti</td><td></td></tr>
<tr><td></td><td>Murtha</td><td></td></tr>
<tr><td>mri</td><td>Marigold</td><td></td></tr>
<tr><td>mrl</td><td>Merville</td><td></td></tr>
<tr><td>mrn</td><td>Morna</td><td></td></tr>
<tr><td></td><td>Myrna</td><td></td></tr>
<tr><td>mro</td><td>Merton</td><td></td></tr>
<tr><td>mrs</td><td>Marsden</td><td></td></tr>
<tr><td>mrt</td><td>Marston</td><td></td></tr>
<tr><td>mrv</td><td>Marvellous</td><td></td></tr>
<tr><td>msa</td><td>Marson</td><td></td></tr>
<tr><td></td><td>Mason</td><td></td></tr>
<tr><td>mua</td><td>Moray</td><td></td></tr>
<tr><td></td><td>Morey</td><td></td></tr>
<tr><td></td><td>Murray</td><td></td></tr>
<tr><td></td><td>Murry</td><td></td></tr>
<tr><td>mud</td><td>Murchadh</td><td></td></tr>
<tr><td></td><td>Murdo</td><td></td></tr>
<tr><td></td><td>Murdoch</td><td></td></tr>
<tr><td></td><td>Murtagh</td><td></td></tr>
<tr><td>mui</td><td>Muir</td><td></td></tr>
<tr><td>mun</td><td>Munga</td><td></td></tr>
<tr><td></td><td>Mungo</td><td></td></tr>
<tr><td>muo</td><td>Monro</td><td></td></tr>
<tr><td></td><td>Munro</td><td></td></tr>
<tr><td>mur</td><td>Meral</td><td>may</td></tr>
<tr><td></td><td>Merall</td><td>mev</td></tr>
<tr><td></td><td>Merel</td><td></td></tr>
<tr><td></td><td>Meriel</td><td></td></tr>
<tr><td></td><td>Merilyn</td><td></td></tr>
<tr><td></td><td>Meriol</td><td></td></tr>
<tr><td></td><td>Merriel</td><td></td></tr>
<tr><td></td><td>Merril</td><td></td></tr>
</table>

<table>
<tr><td></td><td>Meryl</td><td></td></tr>
<tr><td></td><td>Muriel</td><td></td></tr>
<tr><td></td><td>Murrell</td><td></td></tr>
<tr><td>mva</td><td>Mabyn</td><td></td></tr>
<tr><td></td><td>Maeve</td><td></td></tr>
<tr><td></td><td>Maven</td><td></td></tr>
<tr><td></td><td>Mavin</td><td></td></tr>
<tr><td></td><td>Mavon</td><td></td></tr>
<tr><td>mye</td><td>Myer</td><td></td></tr>
<tr><td></td><td>Myers</td><td></td></tr>
<tr><td>myn</td><td>Manard</td><td></td></tr>
<tr><td></td><td>Maynard</td><td></td></tr>
<tr><td>myt</td><td>Myrtilla</td><td></td></tr>
<tr><td></td><td>Myrtle</td><td></td></tr>
<tr><td>naa</td><td>Nayland</td><td></td></tr>
<tr><td>nab</td><td>Naboth</td><td></td></tr>
<tr><td>nad</td><td>Nada</td><td>ber</td></tr>
<tr><td></td><td>Nadene</td><td></td></tr>
<tr><td></td><td>Nadia</td><td></td></tr>
<tr><td></td><td>Nadine</td><td></td></tr>
<tr><td></td><td>Nadyn</td><td></td></tr>
<tr><td></td><td>Nydia</td><td></td></tr>
<tr><td>nah</td><td>Napthali</td><td></td></tr>
<tr><td>nal</td><td>Natache</td><td>joa</td></tr>
<tr><td></td><td>Natalia</td><td></td></tr>
<tr><td></td><td>Natalie</td><td></td></tr>
<tr><td></td><td>Natasha</td><td></td></tr>
<tr><td></td><td>Natelie</td><td></td></tr>
<tr><td></td><td>Nathalie</td><td></td></tr>
<tr><td></td><td>Natty</td><td></td></tr>
<tr><td></td><td>Tasha</td><td></td></tr>
<tr><td>nam</td><td>Nahum</td><td></td></tr>
<tr><td>nao</td><td>Naomi</td><td></td></tr>
<tr><td></td><td>Naomia</td><td></td></tr>
<tr><td></td><td>Naomie</td><td></td></tr>
<tr><td></td><td>Neomi</td><td></td></tr>
<tr><td>nap</td><td>Nap</td><td></td></tr>
<tr><td></td><td>Napoleon</td><td></td></tr>
<tr><td>nar</td><td>Narcissus</td><td></td></tr>
<tr><td>nas</td><td>Naseem</td><td></td></tr>
<tr><td>nat</td><td>Nasham</td><td></td></tr>
<tr><td></td><td>Nat</td><td></td></tr>
<tr><td></td><td>Nath</td><td></td></tr>
<tr><td></td><td>Natha</td><td></td></tr>
<tr><td></td><td>Nathan</td><td></td></tr>
<tr><td></td><td>Nathanael</td><td></td></tr>
<tr><td></td><td>Nathaneell</td><td></td></tr>
<tr><td></td><td>Nathanel</td><td></td></tr>
<tr><td></td><td>Nathanial</td><td></td></tr>
<tr><td></td><td>Nathaniel</td><td></td></tr>
</table>

<table>
<tr><td></td><td>Nathaniell</td><td></td></tr>
<tr><td></td><td>Nathanil</td><td></td></tr>
<tr><td></td><td>Nathanl</td><td></td></tr>
<tr><td></td><td>Nathl</td><td></td></tr>
<tr><td>nay</td><td>Naismith</td><td></td></tr>
<tr><td></td><td>Nasmith</td><td></td></tr>
<tr><td></td><td>Naysmith</td><td></td></tr>
<tr><td>nea</td><td>Neva</td><td></td></tr>
<tr><td>neb</td><td>Newby</td><td></td></tr>
<tr><td>ned</td><td>Nerida</td><td>ane</td></tr>
<tr><td></td><td>Nerina</td><td></td></tr>
<tr><td></td><td>Nerissa</td><td></td></tr>
<tr><td>neh</td><td>Neh</td><td></td></tr>
<tr><td></td><td>Nehemiah</td><td></td></tr>
<tr><td></td><td>Nem</td><td></td></tr>
<tr><td></td><td>Nemiah</td><td></td></tr>
<tr><td></td><td>Nemiath</td><td></td></tr>
<tr><td>nei</td><td>Nail</td><td>hel</td></tr>
<tr><td></td><td>Neal</td><td></td></tr>
<tr><td></td><td>Neil</td><td></td></tr>
<tr><td></td><td>Neill</td><td></td></tr>
<tr><td></td><td>Neilson</td><td></td></tr>
<tr><td></td><td>Nel</td><td></td></tr>
<tr><td></td><td>Nele</td><td></td></tr>
<tr><td></td><td>Nelson</td><td></td></tr>
<tr><td></td><td>Niall</td><td></td></tr>
<tr><td></td><td>Niel</td><td></td></tr>
<tr><td></td><td>Nielson</td><td></td></tr>
<tr><td></td><td>Nigal</td><td></td></tr>
<tr><td></td><td>Nigel</td><td></td></tr>
<tr><td></td><td>Nilsen</td><td></td></tr>
<tr><td>nep</td><td>Neptune</td><td></td></tr>
<tr><td>ner</td><td>Nerys</td><td></td></tr>
<tr><td>net</td><td>Newton</td><td></td></tr>
<tr><td>nev</td><td>Nevell</td><td></td></tr>
<tr><td></td><td>Nevil</td><td></td></tr>
<tr><td></td><td>Nevile</td><td></td></tr>
<tr><td></td><td>Nevill</td><td></td></tr>
<tr><td></td><td>Neville</td><td></td></tr>
<tr><td>new</td><td>Newman</td><td></td></tr>
<tr><td>nic</td><td>Cailean</td><td>clm</td></tr>
<tr><td></td><td>Colan</td><td>dom</td></tr>
<tr><td></td><td>Coleen</td><td>ver</td></tr>
<tr><td></td><td>Colen</td><td></td></tr>
<tr><td></td><td>Colet</td><td></td></tr>
<tr><td></td><td>Colette</td><td></td></tr>
<tr><td></td><td>Colin</td><td></td></tr>
<tr><td></td><td>Colina</td><td></td></tr>
<tr><td></td><td>Colleen</td><td></td></tr>
<tr><td></td><td>Collen</td><td></td></tr>
</table>

	Collette	
	Collin	
	Coulson	
	Coulton	
	Nic	
	Nichalos	
	Nichelas	
	Nichol	
	Nicholas	
	Nicholaus	
	Nicholson	
	Nichs	
	Nick	
	Nickallus	
	Nickola	
	Nickolas	
	Nicodemas	
	Nicol	
	Nicola	
	Nicolas	
	Nicolaus	
	Nicole	
	Nicolet	
	Nicolette	
	Nicoya	
	Nikola	
	Nocolas	
	Nycholas	
	Nycolas	
	Nycolis	
nim	**Nimrod**	
nin	**Nineon**	ann
	Ninia	
	Ninian	
	Nynia	
niv	Nevan	
	Neves	
	Nevin	
	Nevis	
	Niven	
	Nivian	
noa	**Noah**	
nob	**Noble**	
noe	Newel	
	Newell	
	Noel	
	Noella	
	Noelle	
	Nowel	
nol	**Nolan**	

	Nolen	
non	Anocea	
	Anona	
	Nona	
nor	Norfold	
	Norice	
	Noris	
	Norma	
	Norman	
	Norna	
	Norreys	
	Norrie	
	Norris	
	Norriss	
	Norton	
	Tormod	
not	**Nottingham**	
nou	**Norbut**	
nov	**Norval**	
	Norville	
oat	**Oates**	
oba	**Obadiah**	
	Obed	
	Obediah	
	Obidiah	
obe	**Obedience**	
oce	**Ocean**	
oct	Octavia	
	Octavious	
	Octavius	
	Octavus	
	Tary	
	Tave	
	Tavie	
odo	Odette	
	Odille	
	Odo	
	Othi	
	Otho	
	Oti	
	Otis	
	Ottilia	
	Otto	
ogd	**Ogden**	
ola	Auley	hum
	Olaf	oli
	Olave	
oli	Livie	hel
	Nola	ola
	Noll	

	Nollie	
	Oliff	
	Oliffe	
	Oliva	
	Olive	
	Oliver	
	Olivette	
	Olivia	
	Ollett	
	Ollie	
	Olliver	
oln	**Olinda**	
oly	**Olympia**	
	Olympias	
oma	**Omar**	
ome	**Omega**	
oph	**Ophelia**	
org	**Original**	
ori	Aurora	
	Oriana	
orl	**Orla**	
	Orlagh	
orm	**Ormerod**	
	Ormrod	
orn	Oran	
	Oren	
	Orin	
	Orinda	
	Orrin	
oro	**Ormond**	
orp	**Orpah**	
	Orpha	
	Orphy	
ors	**Orson**	
orv	Orval	
	Orville	
	Orwell	
osb	**Osborn**	
	Osborne	
	Osbourne	
	Osburne	
osc	**Oscar**	osm
	Oscilla	osw
	Osgar	
	Osias	
	Ossie	
	Osyth	
	Ozzy	
osi	**Oswin**	
osm	Osman	osc

Codes giving Variants

Code	Name	Var.
	Osmond	
	Osmund	
osw	**Oswald**	
	Oswall	
	Osweld	
	Oswell	
	Oswold	
	Waldo	
pae	Page	
	Paget	
	Paige	
pag	**Pagan**	
	Payn	
pah	Parthena	
	Parthenia	
	Parthina	
	Parthine	
	Pathania	
	Pathena	
	Pathenia	
	Pathina	
	Theny	
pai	Pacience	pat
	Paitence	
	Patiance	
	Patience	
	Patient	
	Patientia	
pal	**Palmer**	
pam	Pam	
	Pamala	
	Pamela	
	Pamelia	
	Pamila	
	Pamilia	
	Pamilla	
	Pammy	
pan	**Pansy**	
par	Park	
	Parker	
pas	Pascel	
	Pascoe	
	Pask	
pat	Packy	mat
	Pad	pai
	Paddy	pet
	Padraig	
	Paris	
	Partick	
	Partrick	
	Pat	
	Patarick	
	Paterick	
	Paterson	
	Patk	
	Patrek	
	Patric	
	Patricia	
	Patrick	
	Patrik	
	Patrike	
	Patsy	
	Patt	
	Pattie	
	Patty	
	Tricia	
	Trish	
pau	Palina	lyn
	Paul	may
	Paula	
	Pauleen	
	Paulette	
	Paulina	
	Pauline	
	Paull	
	Paulus	
	Pawell	
	Pawl	
	Pawle	
	Pol	
pax	**Paxton**	
pea	**Peace**	
pec	**Pentecost**	
ped	**Perdita**	
pee	**Peregrine**	pet
	Perring	
	Perry	
	Pery	
peh	**Perchance**	
pei	**Precious**	
pel	**Pelham**	
pen	**Pen**	fen
	Penelly	
	Penelope	
	Peninnah	
	Penny	
pep	**Perpetua**	
per	Perceval	
	Perceyvall	
	Percival	
	Percivall	
	Percy	
	Percyvall	
	Percywall	
pes	**Persis**	
pet	Parnel	pat
	Parnell	pee
	Peadair	peu
	Pearse	
	Pearson	
	Peater	
	Peder	
	Peeter	
	Peirce	
	Perina	
	Perkin	
	Pernel	
	Peronelle	
	Peta	
	Pete	
	Peter	
	Petere	
	Peternel	
	Petra	
	Petre	
	Petri	
	Petria	
	Petrice	
	Petronella	
	Petrus	
	Petter	
	Pettor	
	Pierce	
	Piercy	
	Pierre	
	Piers	
	Piran	
	Potter	
	Pter	
	Pyrs	
	Pyttar	
peu	**Pet**	pet
	Petula	
pey	**Peyton**	
pha	**Pharaoh**	
	Pharoah	
phe	Fabethy	
	Faby	
	Feabe	
	Feaby	

	Febee			Philpot			Pleasant	
	Febey			Pip		plt	**Plato**	
	Feby			Pippa		pop	**Poppy**	
	Phabe		phl	**Philander**		por	**Porter**	
	Phaebe		phn	**Phineas**		pos	**Posthumus**	
	Pheabe			Phinehas		pot	**Portia**	
	Pheaby		pho	Filomana	phi	pov	Pov	
	Pheba			Filomena			**Povah**	
	Phebe			Philamon		prc	**Prince**	
	Phebey			Philemon			Princess	
	Pheboe			Philimon		pre	**Preston**	
	Pheby			**Philomena**		pri	**Primrose**	
	Pheebe		phy	Amfelice	phi		Primula	
	Pheeby			Amophless		prn	**Prunella**	
	Pheobe			Amphelice			Purnella	
	Pheoby			Amphelicia		pro	**Protasia**	
	Phiebe			Amphelisia			Prothesa	
	Phob			Amphillis		prs	Cilla	sil
	Phobe			Amphlis			Persilla	
	Phoby			Amphliss			Precila	
	Phoeba			Amphyllis			Precilla	
	Phoebe			Amplena			Prescilla	
	Phoebea			Amples			Pricella	
	Phoebey			Amplias			Pricila	
	Phoebia			Amplis			Pricilla	
	Phoeby			Ampliss			Prisca	
phi	Filbert	dep		Felice			Priscella	
	Fulbert	pho		Felicia			Priscila	
	Phelyp	phy		Felicity			**Priscilla**	
	Phil			Felix			Priscillia	
	Phila			Felles			Prisila	
	Philbert			Fillida			Prisilla	
	Philby			Fillis			Prissie	
	Philibert			Hamphris			Prissila	
	Philip			Hampless			Prissilla	
	Philipa			Hampliss			Prissillo	
	Philipe			Phelim			Prissulla	
	Philiph			Phelise			Prisulla	
	Philipinna			Philis			Scilla	
	Philipp			Philles		prt	**Priestley**	
	Philippa			Phillida		pru	Pru	
	Philippus			Phillis			Prudance	
	Phillapa			Phills			Prudce	
	Phillip			Phillys			**Prudence**	
	Phillipa			Phylis			Prudens	
	Phillipe			**Phyllis**			Prudhence	
	Phillipp		pia	**Pia**			Prudie	
	Phillippa		pic	**Pickles**			Prue	
	Phillup		pla	**Plaxy**		prv	**Providence**	
	Philly		ple	**Pleasance**		pto	**Ptomely**	

98

Codes giving Variants

pur	**Pure**			Ralfe		rea	**Read**	
	Purina			**Ralph**			Reed	
que	**Quentin**			Ralphe			Reid	
	Quincy			Ralphie		reb	Becca	
	Quinn			Ralphina			Beccy	
	Quintin			Raoul			Beck	
	Quinton			Raph			Becky	
qun	**Queen**			Raphe			Reb	
	Queenie			Rauf			Reba	
	Reine			Rauffe			Rebacca	
rac	Racey	shi		Raul			Rebackah	
	Rachael	ray		Rayfe			Rebbeca	
	Rachal			Rodolph			Rebbecca	
	Rachall			Rodolphus			Rebbie	
	Racheal			Rodulph			Rebe	
	Rachel			Rolf			Rebeca	
	Rachele			Rollo			Rebecah	
	Rachell			Rolph			Rebecay	
	Racherl			Rudd			**Rebecca**	
	Rachil			Rudolf			Rebeccah	
	Rachill			Rudolph			Rebecha	
	Rachl			Rudy			Rebecka	
	Rachle		ram	**Ramsden**			Rebeckah	
	Rae		ran	Rand	mir		Rebeckey	
	Ralchel			**Randal**	ral		Rebeka	
	Raonaid			Randall			Rebekah	
	Raquel			Randel			Rebekkah	
	Ratchel			Randell			Reby	
	Ratchell			Randey			Recca	
	Reachal			Randle		red	**Redvers**	
	Reachel			Randol		ree	**Reeve**	
	Rechel			Randolph			Reeves	
	Richel			Randulphus		reg	Gina	ros
rad	Radegon			Randy			Raghnall	row
	Radegund			Ransome			Raine	ver
	Radigall			Ranulf			Ranald	
rae	**Raleigh**		rap	Rafael	ral		Rayner	
raf	**Radford**			**Raphael**			Reg	
rai	**Radcliff**			Raphaela			Reggie	
ral	Radolph	ran	ras	**Ralston**			Regina	
	Radolphe	rap	rat	**Ratcliffe**			**Reginald**	
	Radolphus	rol	raw	**Rawdon**			Regnold	
	Radulphi		ray	Ramona	rac		Reighnolde	
	Radulphus			Ramond			Rex	
	Rafe			Ray			Reynard	
	Raff			**Raymond**			Reynaud	
	Raffe			Raymonde			Reynold	
	Raiph			Raymund			Ron	
	Raiphe			Reamonn			Ronald	
	Ralf			Redmond			Rondle	

	Ronnie	
rej	**Rejoice**	
	Rejoyce	
ren	**Renfred**	
	Renfry	
rep	**Repent**	
reu	**Reuben**	ben
	Reubena	
	Reubin	
	Reubon	
	Reupen	
	Reuven	
	Rheuben	
	Rhuben	
	Rube	
	Ruben	
	Rubie	
	Rubin	
	Rubina	
	Rubuen	
	Ruby	
	Rubyna	
	Rueben	
	Ruiben	
rhe	Rea	and
	Rhea	may
	Ria	
rhi	**Rhian**	
	Rhiannon	
rhn	**Rhonda**	
rho	Rhoada	rod
	Rhoades	roe
	Rhoda	
	Rhodah	
	Rhode	
	Rhodes	
	Rhody	
	Roda	
	Rode	
	Rodha	
rhy	Price	
	Pryce	
	Reece	
	Rees	
	Reese	
	Rhys	
	Rice	
ric	Dick	der
	Dickinson	
	Dickon	

	Dixon	
	Hick	
	Hicket	
	Hitch	
	Hudde	
	Hudson	
	Rchard	
	Ri	
	Ric	
	Ricard	
	Ricardi	
	Ricardo	
	Ricardus	
	Ricd	
	Rich	
	Richa	
	Richad	
	Richanda	
	Richard	
	Richarde	
	Richardi	
	Richardson	
	Richardus	
	Richd	
	Richdus	
	Richeard	
	Richenda	
	Richerd	
	Richi	
	Richie	
	Richmal	
	Richmond	
	Richoard	
	Richrd	
	Richus	
	Rici	
	Rick	
	Ricket	
	Rickey	
	Ricky	
	Ricus	
	Ritchard	
	Ritchie	
	Rychard	
	Rycharde	
	Rychardus	
	Rycherd	
	Rychert	
rid	Ridlay	
	Ridley	

		Ridly	
rig	**Rigby**		
ril	**Riley**		
rip	**Ripley**		
riz	Rispah		
	Rizpah		
rma	**Ramsay**		
	Ramsey		
roa	**Roald**		
rob	Bob	alb	
	Bobbie	bet	
	Bobby	rog	
	Dob	ruf	
	Hab	sab	
	Habby		
	Hob		
	Hobson		
	Hopkin		
	Nob		
	Nobby		
	Rab		
	Rabbie		
	Rabi		
	Rabina		
	Raby		
	Raibeart		
	Raven		
	Rbt		
	Ro		
	Rob		
	Robart		
	Robarte		
	Robartie		
	Robartt		
	Robbert		
	Robbie		
	Robeart		
	Robena		
	Rober		
	Robert		
	Roberta		
	Roberte		
	Roberti		
	Robertina		
	Roberts		
	Robertson		
	Robertt		
	Robertus		
	Robet		
	Robin		

Codes giving Variants

Code	Name	Var1	Var2
	Robina		
	Robinetta		
	Robinson		
	Robr		
	Robrt		
	Robson		
	Robt		
	Robte		
	Robti		
	Robtus		
	Robyn		
	Roy		
	Rupert		
	Ruperta		
roc	Rocco	shi	
	Rochelle		
	Rock		
	Rocky		
rod	Rod	rho	
	Rodney	roe	
roe	Roddie	rho	
	Roddy	rod	
	Roderic	rog	
	Roderick		
	Rodk		
	Rodrick		
	Rody		
	Rory		
	Rotheric		
	Ruairidh		
	Ruiraidh		
	Rurik		
rog	Dodge	rob	
	Hodge	roe	
	Hodgkin		
	Hodgson		
	Hodson		
	Rodger		
	Rogar		
	Rogeni		
	Roger		
	Rogeri		
	Rogerii		
	Rogers		
	Rogher		
	Rojer		
rol	Orlando	ral	
	Rawling		
	Rawson		
	Roland		
	Rolande		
	Rolla		
	Rolland		
	Rolly		
	Rowland		
	Rowlandson		
rom	**Roma**		
	Romaine		
	Romeo		
	Romola		
ron	**Royden**		
	Roydon		
ros	Ffion	lyn	
	Roanne	reg	
	Roas	rso	
	Rois		
	Roisin		
	Rosa		
	Rosabel		
	Rosabell		
	Rosaleen		
	Rosalia		
	Rosalie		
	Rosalina		
	Rosalind		
	Rosalinda		
	Rosaline		
	Rosalyn		
	Rosamond		
	Rosamund		
	Rosan		
	Rosana		
	Rosanah		
	Rosanan		
	Rosann		
	Rosanna		
	Rosannae		
	Rosannah		
	Rose		
	Rosea		
	Roseana		
	Roseand		
	Roseann		
	Roseanna		
	Roseannah		
	Roseanne		
	Rosehannah		
	Roselia		
	Roselin		
	Roseline		
	Rosella		
	Rosemary		
	Rosemond		
	Rosemund		
	Rosena		
	Rosenia		
	Roseta		
	Rosetta		
	Rosette		
	Rosey		
	Roshannah		
	Rosheen		
	Rosie		
	Rosiland		
	Rosilla		
	Rosilyn		
	Rosimond		
	Rosina		
	Rosita		
	Roslin		
	Roslyn		
	Rosomond		
	Rossalyn		
	Rossella		
	Rosser		
	Rossetta		
	Rossette		
	Rosy		
	Royce		
	Roza		
	Rozalyn		
	Rozanna		
	Rozina		
	Zetta		
row	Raewyn	reg	
	Rhona		
	Rhonwen		
	Rohan		
	Rona		
	Rowan		
	Rowe		
	Rowena		
rox	**Roxana**		
	Roxie		
roy	Roystan		
	Royston		
rso	**Ross**	ros	
	Rosslyn		
ruf	Rufe	rob	
	Rufus		

code	name	var		code	name	var		code	name	var
rus	Russ	cyu			Samuelis				Sary	
	Russel				Samuell				Sarye	
	Russell				Samuiel				Sera	
	Rusty				Samul				Serah	
rut	**Ruth**				Samule				Sorcha	
	Ruthe				Samulel				Srah	
	Ruthie				Samvell				Zara	
	Ruthven				Samwell				Zarita	
rwo	**Rowley**				Somerled				Zora	
rya	**Ryan**		san	**Samantha**	sam			Zuhra	
ryo	**Royal**		sao	**Salmon**		sas	Sampson	sam
	Royalyn		sap	Saphira			**Samson**	
	Royle			Sapphira			Sanson	
saa	**Salathiel**			**Sapphire**		sat	**Sabath**	
sab	Bina	rob	sar	Mor	shr	sau	**Saul**	sol
	Binah	sai		Morag		sav	Salvador	
	Sabeeha			Sadie			**Salvator**	
	Sabin			Saidee			Salvatore	
	Sabina			Sal		sax	**Saxon**	
	Sabinah			Salla		say	Saer	
	Sabine			Salley			**Sayer**	
	Savina			Sally		sbe	Seabright	
	Sebina			Saly			**Sebert**	
sac	**Sacheveral**			Sar		sca	**Scarlet**	
sad	**Sadler**			Sara			Scarlett	
sag	Sargant			Sarae		sch	**Scholastica**	
	Sargeant			Saragh		sco	**Scott**	
	Sargent			**Sarah**		sdi	**Sidwell**	
	Sarjeant			Saraha		sea	**Sewal**	
	Sarjent			Sarahae			Sewell	
	Sergeant			Sarahan		seb	Bastian	
sai	Sabara	sab		Sarahann			Seb	
	Sabra			Sarai			Seba	
	Sabrah			Saraid			**Sebastian**	
	Sabrina			Saram		sec	**Secundus**	
	Seabra			Saran		sed	**Seward**	
	Sebra			Saranna		see	**Serle**	
sam	Sam	san		Sarar		sef	**Sefton**	
	Samarie	sas		Saray		seh	**Selah**	
	Samella			Sarayh		sel	Selbey	
	Samentha			Sareh			**Selby**	
	Sameull			Sarena		sen	**Seaton**	
	Samewel			Sarey			Seton	
	Samewell			Sarh		seo	Serena	may
	Saml			Sarha			Serenah	
	Samll			Sariah			**Sereno**	
	Sammuel			Sarina			Serenus	
	Sammy			Sarinah			Serina	
	Samual			Sarita		sep	September	
	Samuel			Sarrah			Septima	

code	name	variant
	Septimas	
	Septimus	
ser	**Seraphina**	
	Seraphita	
set	**Seth**	
	Syth	
sew	Selvin	sul
	Selwyn	
	Sulwen	
	Sulwyn	
sex	Sexa	
	Sextus	
sey	Seamark	
	Seamor	
	Seamore	
	Seamour	
	Seymour	
sga	**Sagar**	
sha	Shadrac	
	Shadrach	
	Shadrack	
	Shudrach	
shc	**Shackleton**	
shd	Sherida	
	Sheridan	
she	Shephard	
	Shepherd	
	Sheppard	
shi	Shelley	cec
	Shelly	rac
	Sher	roc
	Shirlene	
	Shirley	
	Shirly	
	Shurley	
shl	**Shelton**	
sho	**Sholto**	
shp	**Sharp**	
	Sharpe	
shr	**Sharon**	cha
	Sharry	sar
	Sheron	
shw	**Shaw**	
sia	**Signatora**	
sib	Cibill	
	Cybil	
	Sebell	
	Sib	
	Sibbilla	
	Sibby	

code	name	variant
	Sibella	
	Sibley	
	Sibly	
	Sibyl	
	Sibylla	
	Sybbell	
	Sybel	
	Sybella	
	Sybil	
	Sybill	
sic	**Silence**	
	Sill	
	Tace	
	Tacey	
	Tacye	
sid	Cydney	
	Seodina	
	Sid	
	Siddy	
	Sidney	
	Sidonia	
	Sidony	
	Sudney	
	Sydney	
	Sydonah	
	Sydonia	
	Syndonia	
sie	**Siegfried**	
sig	Sig	sim
	Sigismund	
	Sigmund	
sil	Sila	cec
	Silas	lav
	Sileas	prs
	Silias	
	Silueness	
	Silva	
	Silvanus	
	Silvas	
	Silvenus	
	Silvester	
	Silvey	
	Silvia	
	Sylvan	
	Sylvanus	
	Sylvester	
	Sylvia	
	Sylvina	
sim	Sim	sig
	Simean	

code	name	variant
	Simeon	
	Simieon	
	Simion	
	Simon	
	Simond	
	Simonde	
	Simone	
	Simpson	
	Simund	
	Sym	
	Symo	
	Symon	
	Symond	
sin	**Sinclair**	
sir	Sigerith	
	Sigrid	
	Sirida	
siw	**Siward**	
slo	**Sloane**	
smi	**Smith**	
	Smyth	
sno	**Snowdrop**	
sol	Salamon	sau
	Saloma	
	Salome	
	Sol	
	Solly	
	Soloman	
	Solomon	
	Zollie	
sop	Saphia	eli
	Sofia	
	Sonia	
	Sonya	
	Soph	
	Sopha	
	Sophi	
	Sophia	
	Sophiah	
	Sophie	
	Sophy	
	Sopia	
sor	**Soraya**	
spe	Spence	
	Spencer	
	Spenser	
squ	**Squire**	
sri	**Sir**	
sta	Stan	
	Stanby	

Code	Name	Extra
	Stanhope	
	Stanley	
std	**Stodart**	
ste	Sephen	
	Staphen	
	Steaphen	
	Steaven	
	Steephen	
	Stefan	
	Stepen	
	Stephan	
	Stephana	
	Stephane	
	Stephani	
	Stephania	
	Stephanie	
	Stephanus	
	Stephen	
	Stephenson	
	Stepheus	
	Stephie	
	Stephn	
	Stepn	
	Stev	
	Steve	
	Steven	
	Stevens	
	Stevyn	
	Stifania	
stf	**Stafford**	
sti	Sterling	
	Stirling	
stk	**Starkie**	
stm	**Stimpson**	
stn	**Stanislas**	
sto	Stamford	
	Stanford	
str	**Stratford**	
stt	**Stanton**	
stw	Stew	
	Steward	
	Stewart	
	Stuart	
sug	**Sugden**	
sul	**Sullivan**	sew
	Sully	
sus	Shusan	ann
	Shusanna	
	Suan	
	Suana	

Code	Name
	Suanh
	Suannah
	Sue
	Suhannah
	Suke
	Sukey
	Sukie
	Suky
	Sus
	Susa
	Susahnah
	Susan
	Susana
	Susanae
	Susanah
	Susanay
	Susand
	Susaner
	Susanh
	Susanha
	Susann
	Susanna
	Susannah
	Susanne
	Susanney
	Susey
	Sush
	Sushana
	Sushanah
	Sushannah
	Susie
	Suson
	Sussan
	Sussana
	Sussanah
	Sussanna
	Sussannah
	Susy
	Suzan
	Suzana
	Suzanna
	Suzannah
	Suzanne
	Zsa
	Zusi
sut	**Sutcliffe**
sva	Savil
	Savile
	Savill
	Savilla

Code	Name	Extra
swa	Swailey	
	Swales	
	Swaley	
swi	Swindeniah	
	Swithin	
	Swithun	
swn	**Swinbourne**	
	Swinburne	
swr	**Swire**	
tab	Tabatha	
	Tabby	
	Tabetha	
	Tabez	
	Tabitha	
	Tabotha	
tae	**Tate**	
tai	**Talitha**	
tal	**Talbot**	
tam	Tamah	daa
	Tamar	tho
	Tamara	
	Tamer	
	Tamor	
	Tamyra	
	Tayma	
	Thamar	
tan	**Tancred**	
tar	**Tara**	
tas	**Tansy**	
tat	Tana	ant
	Tanis	
	Tanya	
	Tatiana	
	Tonya	
tau	**Tallulah**	
tay	**Taylor**	
tea	**Teasdale**	
tee	**Tempest**	
teg	**Tegwen**	
	Tegwyn	
tel	**Telford**	
tem	**Temperance**	
	Temperence	
ten	Tenant	
	Tennant	
tep	**Temple**	
ter	Terance	cha
	Terasa	edw
	Terena	est
	Terence	

Codes giving Variants

	Teresa		**thi**	**Thalia**				Tomenia
	Teresia		**thk**	Thickell				Tomcy
	Teressa			Thirkill				Tomina
	Tereza			**Thorkill**				Tomison
	Terrance			Torcall				Tomlinson
	Terrence			Torquil				Tommina
	Terrie		**thl**	**Thelma**				Tommy
	Terry		**thn**	**Theron**				Tommyson
	Tersia		**tho**	Mace	tam			Tomsen
	Terza			Macey				Tomson
	Tess			Tam				Tos
	Tessa			Tamasin		**thp**	Offy	edw
	Tesse			Tamasine			Theaphilus
	Tessie			Tamazine			Theoph
	Theresa			Tammas			Theophania
	Theresdi			Tammy			Theophelus
	Therese			Tamsin			Theophila
	Theriza			Tamson			Theophili
	Therna			Tamzen			Theophilius
	Thersa			Tho			**Theophilus**
	Thersdi			Thoams			Theophius
	Therza			Thoas			Theophphelous
	Thirsa			Thom			Theoples
	Thirza			Thoma			Tiffany
	Thirzar			Thomae		**thr**	**Thermuthis**
	Thursa			Thomalin		**tht**	**Thornton**
	Thursey			Thomam		**thu**	Thorston
	Thurza			**Thomas**			**Thurstan**
	Thyrsa			Thomasin			Thursten
	Thyrza			Thomasina			Thurston
	Tirza			Thomasine			Turstan
	Tirzah			Thomason		**thy**	Thora
	Tracie			Thomat			**Thyra**
	Tracy			Thomazen			Tyra
	Trecesea			Thomazin		**til**	**Tilden**
	Tresa			Thomazine		**tim**	Tad
	Treza			Thome			Tadhgh
	Turlough			Thomenia			Teague
tet	**Tertius**			Thomison			Teige
tey	Tenny	den		Thomizon			Thad
	Tennyson			Thommas			Thaddeus
tha	**Thekla**			Thompson			Thaddius
thd	**Thorold**			Thoms			Thimothy
	Torold			Thomson			Thimsy
the	Tedbald	edw		Thos			Tim
	Tedbar			Ths			Timmy
	Teubald			Tom			Timoth
	Theobald			Tomas			Timothe
	Tibald			Tomasin			Timotheus
thf	**Thrift**			Tomasine			Timothey

	Timothia	uni	Unity			**Verity**		
	Timothy	upt	**Upton**	vel	Verley		
	Timy	ura	Urana		**Verlie**		
tit	**Titus**		**Urania**	ven	Verna		
tob	Tobe	urb	Arban		Verney		
	Tobiah		**Urban**		Vernie		
	Tobias	urh	**Urith**		**Vernon**		
	Tobin	uri	Urena	ver	Feroniaca	bei
	Tobit		Uria		Vera	may
	Toby		**Uriah**		Vere	nic
toh	**Thorley**		Urina		Verena	reg
	Thornley	url	**Uriel**		Verona	
top	**Topsy**	urn	**Urian**		**Veronica**	
tor	**Troy**		Urien	ves	Vessy	
tra	Travers	urs	Ulla		Vest	
	Travis		Ursiley		**Vesta**	
tre	Trefor		**Ursula**	veu	**Venus**	
	Treva		Vrsula	via	Vidal	
	Treveens	uzz	**Uzziah**		Viel	
	Trevor	vac	**Vance**		**Vitalis**	
tri	**Trinity**	vad	**Valda**	vic	Vic	
tro	**Troth**		Velda		Vick	
	Trothe	vah	**Vashti**		Vickers	
trs	Tristan	val	Val		Vicky	
	Tristram		Valantine		**Victor**	
trt	Traiton		Valarie		Victoria	
	Trayton		Valatine		Victorine	
tru	**Truman**		Valence		Vita	
try	Fryphena		Valencia	vie	**Vine**	
	Trephena		Valentia	vig	**Virgil**	
	Triffie		Valentina	vin	Vince	lav
	Triphena		Valentine		**Vincent**	
	Triphosa		Valeria		Vincentia	
	Tryphena		Valerian		Vinny	
	Tryphoena		**Valerie**	vio	Vi	
	Tryphon	van	Nessa		**Viola**	
	Tryphosa		Van		Violet	
tun	**Turner**		Vane		Violetta	
tur	**True**		**Vanessa**		Voilet	
tyl	Tyler		Vennice		Yalonda	
tyr	**Tyrone**		Venyce		Yola	
uch	**Uchtred**		Venyse		Yolande	
	Ughtred	vas	Vancelo	vir	Ginger	eug
ulr	**Ulric**		**Vanslow**		Ginnie	gue
	Ulrica	vau	**Vaughan**		Vergenie	joa
uly	Lyss	ved	Verdon		Virgie	
	Uileos		**Verdun**		Virgina	
	Ulick	vee	Vanetta		**Virginia**	
	Ullace		**Venetia**	vit	**Virtue**	
	Ulysses	vei	Verita	viv	Bibby	

106

	Bibiana		wes	**Wesley**			Gwilym
	Fithian			Wesly			Helma
	Phythian			West			Hilma
	Vian			Westley			Ilma
	Vivian			Westly			Liam
	Vivien		wet	**Weston**			Mina
	Vivienne			Whiston			Minadab
	Vyvian		wha	Warton			Minella
	Vyvyan			**Wharton**			Minette
waa	**Wallace**	wal	whe	**Wheatley**			Minie
	Wallis		whi	Whitmee			Minna
	Wally			**Whitney**			Minnie
	Whalley			Witney			Uillean
wad	**Waldeve**		wht	**Whittaker**			Valma
	Waldive		wib	**Wilbert**	alb		Velma
wae	**Wade**			Wilbur	wil		Vilma
waf	**Walford**			Wilby			Walliam
wai	**Wainwright**		wid	**Windsor**			Welmot
wak	**Walker**		wif	**Wilford**			Wilhelm
wal	Gwallter	waa	wih	**Winthrop**			Wilhelmi
	Gwalter		wil	Amina	ans		Wilhelmina
	Wal			Aminadab	may		Wilhelmus
	Wallter			Aminah	wib		Wilhilmina
	Walt			Bill	wlf		Wiliam
	Walter			Billie			Wilkinson
	Wat			Billy			Will
	Water			Billyanna			Willa
	Waters			Bleyana			Willaim
	Watkin			Blihanna			Willam
	Watson			Elma			Willeam
	Watt			Elmore			Willelmus
	Watter			Elmy			Willem
	Watty			Guglielma			Willhelmina
	Whalter			Guilielmus			Willhimina
wan	Vanda	gue		Guilihelmi			Willi
	Wanda			Gul			Willia
war	Warin			Gulelmus			**William**
	Warner			Guliel			Williame
was	**Washington**			Gulielimus			Williamina
wat	**Walton**			Guliell			Williams
wav	**Wave**			Guliellmi			Williamson
	Waverly			Guliellmus			Williamus
waw	Warick			Gulielm			Willian
	Warwick			Gulielmi			Willie
way	Wain			Gulielmu			Willielmi
	Wayne			Gulielmum			Willielmus
web	**Webster**			Gulielmus			Willim
wee	**Welberry**			Gulih			Willimi
wel	**Wellington**			Gulmi			Willims
wen	**Wendy**			Gwilliam			Willimus

Code	Name	Var
	Willis	
	Willm	
	Willmi	
	Willms	
	Willmus	
	Wills	
	Willum	
	Willus	
	Willy	
	Willyam	
	Wilm	
	Wilma	
	Wilmett	
	Wilmi	
	Wilmit	
	Wilmot	
	Wilms	
	Wilson	
	Wilyam	
	Wlliam	
	Wm	
	Wylie	
	Wylliam	
	Wyllm	
	Wyllya	
wim	**Wisdom**	
win	Gwenfrewi	agn
	Gwinefried	fre
	Juno	gwe
	Oonagh	wis
	Una	
	Wenifred	
	Wenn	
	Wenny	
	Wimifrid	
	Wineford	
	Winefred	
	Winey	
	Winfred	
	Winiford	
	Winifred	
	Winifridae	
	Winifrith	
	Winnefrid	
	Winney	
	Winnfred	
	Winnie	
	Winnifred	
	Wynethred	
	Wynne	
wio	Willaba	
	Willo	
	Willoby	
	Willoughby	
wis	**Winston**	win
	Winton	
wit	**Wilton**	
wla	**Waller**	
wle	**Wells**	
wlf	Wifred	fre
	Wilf	wil
	Wilfred	
	Wilfrid	
	Wilfridi	
	Wilfridus	
	Willfraie	
wol	**Wolf**	
woo	**Wood**	
	Woodrow	
	Woodward	
wor	Worthey	
	Worthy	
wra	**Ward**	
wri	**Wright**	
wrr	Garnet	
	Wareing	
	Waring	
	Warren	
wyb	**Wybert**	
wyf	Wenford	
	Wynford	
wyn	**Wyndham**	
xan	**Xanthe**	
	Xanthippe	
xav	**Xavier**	
	Xaviera	
	Zavier	
	Zerviah	
yan	**Yancy**	
yor	**Yorick**	
you	**Young**	
zab	**Zabdiel**	
zac	Laccheus	eze
	Zacariah	isa
	Zacarias	
	Zacceus	
	Zacchaeus	
	Zaccheus	
	Zacharia	
	Zachariah	
	Zacharias	
	Zachary	
	Zack	
	Zackariah	
	Zackriah	
	Zak	
	Zake	
	Zechariah	
	Zecheriah	
zad	**Zadok**	
zai	**Zaida**	
	Zayda	
zea	Xenia	
	Zena	
	Zenas	
	Zenda	
	Zina	
zeb	**Zebadiah**	
	Zebedee	
zed	**Zedekiah**	
zen	**Zenobia**	
zep	Zeph	
	Zephaniah	
zer	**Zerrubabel**	
	Zerrubbabel	
zeu	Zabulon	lau
	Zebulan	
	Zebulen	
	Zebulin	
	Zebulon	
	Zebulun	
zia	Tilpah	
	Zilpah	
	Zilpha	
	Zylpha	
zil	Zilah	
	Ziliah	
	Zilla	
	Zillah	
	Zilliah	
	Zylla	
zim	**Zimri**	
zip	Ziporah	
	Zipporah	
	Ziprah	
zit	Zeta	
	Zita	
zoe	**Zoe**	
zon	**Zona**	
zul	**Zuleika**	